NEW BEGINNINGS

NEW BEGINNINGS

*Sold in aid of the Indian Ocean
Tsunami Earthquake Charities*

MARGARET ATWOOD

MAEVE BINCHY

TRACY CHEVALIER

HARLAN COBEN

PAULO COELHO

J. M. COETZEE

NICHOLAS EVANS

MARK HADDON

NICK HORNBY

MARIAN KEYES

STEPHEN KING

ALEXANDER McCALL SMITH

IAN McEWAN

VIKRAM SETH

JOANNA TROLLOPE

SCOTT TUROW

BLOOMSBURY

First published 2005

This collection © 2005 by Bloomsbury Publishing Plc

The copyright of the individual contributions remains with the respective authors.
The acknowledgements on page 239–241 constitute an extension of this
copyright page.

The moral right of the authors has been asserted

Bloomsbury Publishing Plc, 38 Soho Square, London W1D 3HB

A CIP catalogue record for this book is available from the British Library

ISBN 0 7475 8127 4
9780747581277

10 9 8 7 6 5 4 3 2 1

All papers used by Bloomsbury Publishing are natural, recyclable products made
from wood grown in well-managed forests. The manufacturing processes conform
to the environmental regulations of the country of origin.

Printed in Great Britain by Clays Ltd, St Ives plc

www.bloomsbury.com/tsunami

CONTENTS

PREFACE

New Beginnings is a simple idea to raise money for the Indian Ocean tsunami disaster appeal. The project has depended entirely on the talent, generosity and speed of the authors who have contributed their work. They have made possible an unprecedented global publishing event. A huge thank you to all of them for their belief that this book could literally save lives.

I would also like to thank the agents and publishers worldwide for their enthusiasm and unhesitating support in making this happen. The entire chain of publishing has been involved in this project, from the author to the editor to the printer to the distributor to the sales rep to the bookseller. It could not have happened without the staff from Bloomsbury Publishing, all of whom embraced the challenge instantly, and thanks must go to Nigel Newton, Arzu Tahsin, Katie Bond, Ruth Logan, David Ward, Karen Rinaldi, Holly Roberts, Kathleen Farrar and Elizabeth Ruge.

I would like to send a special thanks to journalist Ben Brown, whose reports for the BBC made me feel that this project was a necessity. *New Beginnings* is dedicated to one of his interviewees, Rohati, who lost her husband and four sons in Aceh. As she clung on to Brown's stiff BBC shoulders, weeping inconsolably, he broke the correspondents' rule of not 'crossing the line' and gave her a hug. For one second there seemed to be some relief in this horror. It is that moment that this book is here to celebrate.

Jonny Geller
Project Director of *New Beginnings*
Managing Director of Curtis Brown (Books)
London, 26th January 2005

FOREWORD

Reading this book is no act of charity. These opening chapters are absolutely compelling, transporting us from the domestic circumstances of Alexander McCall Smith's Edinburgh to behind the net curtains in Marian Keyes' Dublin to the events at the top of a tower block on New Year's Eve in Nick Hornby's London, and on through thirteen other diverse and fascinating worlds. I think that this volume will, unintentionally, make for a greater appreciation of the essential role of a first chapter in setting up the direction and tensions of the novel which follows.

The money raised from the sale of this book worldwide will be given to charities working on both short-term aid and long-term reconstruction in the twelve tsunami-hit countries. Our aim with the UK edition is that all £5.00 of the retail price will be paid through intact to the charities. We have incurred third party costs for printing and paper at base cost but we are currently seeking sponsorship of those costs. If, having bought this book, you are inspired to sponsor these, please e-mail me at N.Newton@bloomsbury.com.

There will be a full public accounting of the money raised on www.bloomsbury.com/tsunami/accounting showing which charities received how much money and when. The book is published on 3rd March 2005 – World Book Day. The first monies will be received in April and will be given immediately to the charities and then monthly thereafter for the one year of the book's intended life.

This book will be published all over the world and the money raised in each country will be given to tsunami charities chosen locally. Bloomsbury USA will give the money raised there to the Save The Children Fund. Our subsidiary in Germany, Berlin Verlag, will give to German UNICEF and their edition will contain leading German authors in addition to the English language authors in this volume. In other countries, foreign language publishers will license it from Bloomsbury and publish it in translation. We will carry their accountings on our website also.

Working on this book, together with Jonny Geller from Curtis Brown, the literary agent whose idea it was, has been inspiring to all of us at Bloomsbury in Soho Square and abroad. Encountering the generosity of our many suppliers and customers in their support of this project has been even more so. To a degree, Bloomsbury owes its existence to the *Live Aid* book which we published at Sidgwick & Jackson in 1984. There I witnessed the motivation that came from being part of an idealistic enterprise in the context of work and it made a deep impression on me at that time when I was deciding to start Bloomsbury. The tsunami has prompted people from many fields of work to rise to great acts of generosity and to donate in kind what they do for a living as part of the relief effort. The fundraising projects from Radio Aid to the Tsunami Benefit concert at the Millennium Stadium in Cardiff to a jazz concert at the 606 Club in London have been inspirational. And all of us are indebted to the real heroes, the aid workers, doctors and nurses who have gone out to the devastated regions to help on the grim frontline.

But heading the list of donors, we must of course thank the sixteen authors who have made this book possible. It has been a privilege to work with these superb writers who have so generously and spontaneously donated their work. I would also like to thank our indefatigable warehouse, Macmillan Distribution, for giving their services free and without hesitation to the complex logistics of this major operation. In turn, may I thank DHL Express whose vans have fanned out across the country delivering these books for free. Our many customers, from independent book-sellers to national bookshop chains, from wholesalers to multiples, from supermarkets and direct sales operations to bookclubs, have all given their support for the launch of this book free of charge. The paper merchants and the printers, Clays, who have had to cope with the huge demand for this book worldwide have given their services at base cost, making no profit. Our bankers, the Royal Bank of Scotland, have made a generous contribution towards the printing costs and we thank them. We are grateful to everyone as £4.82 of the £5.00 retail price is guaranteed to reach the tsunami charities and we hope that the balance of eighteen pence will be raised by the afore-mentioned sponsorship. Finally, I would like to thank you, Reader, because it is your £5.00 we are giving away and you've probably donated money already to the Disasters Emergency Committee since the appeal began in late December, following that harrowing and awful Boxing Day.

This book is dedicated to the people who were there at the time helping each other and to the aid workers who have gone over there. Most of all we remember those who died, were injured or lost loved ones.

Nigel Newton
Chief Executive
Bloomsbury Publishing Plc
London, 26th January 2005

INTRODUCTION BY HELEN FIELDING

The eradication of human life which took place on 26th December 2004 was unimaginable: more than 280,000 people were killed by one geological event. Probably everyone has their own image, moment or story which individualises the horror and the loss. For me it is the father who thought he was holding onto his child as the tsunami hit, then found that all he had left in his hands were her clothes.

That father was a Western tourist. His experience will have been repeated tens of thousands of times along the shores of Africa and Asia. As ever, in the world's poorest regions, when natural disaster strikes there is no ballast. Tens of thousands of families staggering under that sort of grief are now also staring at life with no homes, no facilities and no livelihood.

Many of us have enjoyed the rustic escape from our own reality in beach side idylls now devastated by the tsunami. Parts of the last *Bridget Jones* movie showed Bridget trying to 'find herself' on the coastal islands off Thailand. But the reality of living in such places is vulnerability. The purpose of this book is entirely practical: replacing the losses which can be replaced, rebuilding the aspects of lives which can be rebuilt. No one involved is making any money from it. As near as possible to 100 per cent of takings will go to the charities which have come together to deal with the aftermath of the emergency.

Film stars, sport stars and musicians are familiar champions of causes. But writers are seldom seen on camera, on stage or making pleas in emergency zones. Perhaps it is because writers are so used to observing and commentating on the world that they would overanalyse their own involvement and feel like simplifying fools or phoneys. Perhaps they can't cut their contribution down to the required length without months of missed deadlines and rewriting. Or maybe TV producers just don't want writers at large on their screen, chain smoking with mad hair, in food-stained cardigans.

But here, unusually, writers have come together to publicly give what they can, and to give something rather uncomfortable: work which hasn't been seen yet, first chapters without the rest of the book to back it up.

In the media age, human nature can come across pretty shabbily. One of the glimmers of good which has emerged from the dark times following the tsunami is the startling degree to which people were eager to help. In the great public outpouring of compassion in the wake of the disaster people gave what they could: most often cold hard cash, which is the most useful expression of compassion at such a time. With your – the reader's – help, what the writers have given here will translate into a great deal of cold hard cash, but cash which keeps coming beyond the immediate aftermath, as long as the book stays on the shelves. Thank you for buying this book. Maybe pop out for another copy?

TREE BABY

Margaret Atwood

You remember this. No, you dreamed it. Your dream was of choking, and sinking down, and blankness. You woke from your nightmare and it had already happened. Everything was gone. Everything, and everyone – fathers, mothers, brothers, sisters, the cousins, the tables and chairs and toys and beds – all swept away. Nothing is left of them. Nothing remains but the erased beach and the silence.

There is wreckage. You didn't see that, in your dream. A jumble of smashed years, a heap of broken stories. The stories look like wood and chunks of cement and twisted metal. And sand, a lot of sand. Why is it they say *the sands of time*? You didn't know that yesterday but now you do. You know too much to say. What can be said? Language turns to rubble in your throat.

But look – there's a baby, caught in a treetop, just as in those other dreams, the ones in which you can lift yourself off the earth and fly, and escape the roaring and crashing just behind you. A baby, alive, caught in a green cradle; and it's been rescued, after all. But its name has been lost, along with its tiny past.

What new name will they give it, this child? The one who

1

escaped from your nightmare and floated lightly to a tree, and who looks around itself now with a baby's ordinary amazement? Now time starts up once more, now there is something that can be said: this child must be given a word. A password, a talisman of air, to help it through the many hard gates and shadow doorways ahead. It must be named, again.

Will they call it Catastrophe, will they call it Flotsam, will they call it Sorrow? Will they call it No-Family, will they call it Bereft, will they call it Child-of-a-Tree? Or will they call it Astonishment, or Nevertheless, or Small Mercy?

Or will they call it Beginning?

SOMETHING HAS HAPPENED
Margaret Atwood

Something has happened. But how? Was it overnight, or has it been creeping up on us and we've only just noticed? It's the girls, the young and pretty girls. They used to sing like sirens, like mermaids, all sweet and liquid, breezy melodies, wavy melodies, but now they're shorn of melody, though their mouths open and close as before. Have their tongues been cut out?

This is true as well of the cries of babies, the wailing at funerals, the screams that used to arise, especially at night, from the mad, from the tortured. It's the same thing with the birds: flying as before, spreading out their feathers as before, heads thrown back, beaks gaping, but they're mute. Mute, or muted? Who has been at work, with a great carpet of invisible snow that blots out sound?

Listen: the leaves no longer rustle, the wind no longer sighs, our hearts no longer beat. They've fallen silent. Fallen, as if into the earth. Or is it we who have fallen? Perhaps it's not the world that is soundless but we who are deaf. What membrane seals us off, from the music we used to dance to? Why can't we hear?

BUT IT COULD STILL
Margaret Atwood

Things look bad: I admit it. They look worse than they've looked for years, for centuries. They look the worst ever. Perils loom on all sides. But it could still turn out all right. The baby fell from the eighth-floor balcony but there was a sheepdog underneath that leapt up and caught it in mid-air. A bystander took a picture, it was in the paper. The boy went under for the third time, but the mother – although she was reading a novel – heard a gurgling sound and ran down to the dock, and reached down into the water, and pulled the boy up by his hair, and there was no brain damage. When the explosion occurred the young man was underneath the sink, fixing the plumbing, and so he was not injured. The girl survived the avalanche by making swimming motions with her arms. The father of two-year-old triplets who had cancer in every possible organ watched a lot of comedy films and did Buddhist meditation and went into full remission, where he remains to this day. The airbags actually worked. The cheque did not bounce. The prescription drug company was not lying. The shark nudged the sailor's naked, bleeding leg, then turned away. The rapist got distracted in mid-rape, and his

5

knife and his penis both retracted into him like the soft and delicate horns of a snail, and he went out for a coffee instead. The copy of Darwin's *Origin of Species* the soldier carried next to his heart stopped the oncoming machine-gun bullet. When he said, *My darling, you are the only woman I will adore forever*, he really meant it. As for her, despite the scowling and the cold shoulder and the unanswered phone, it turned out she'd loved him all along.

At this time of year we hunger for such tales. Winter's tales, they are. We want to huddle round them, as if around a small but cheerful fire. The sun sets at four, the temperature plummets, the wind howls, the snow cascades down. Though you nearly froze your fingers off, you did get the tulips planted, just in time. In four months they'll come up, you have faith in that, and they'll look like the picture in the catalogue. In the brown earth there were already hundreds of small green shoots. You didn't know what they were – some sort of little bulb – but there they were, despite everything. What would you call them if they were in a story? Would they be happy endings, or happy beginnings? But they are not in a story, and neither are you. You tucked them back under the mulch and the dead leaves, however. It was the right thing to do on the darkest day.

GEORGIA HALL
Maeve Binchy

Georgia had always been a leader.

Way back at school, she was the one with style. When Georgia decided to carry her school books wrapped up in a red ribbon, everyone else abandoned their schoolbags and satchels and got ribbons also.

It was the same when we arrived at university. She didn't appear to try too hard but everyone wanted to do things her way. She read art history, always saying it was an undemanding thing to do, yet she was at the very top of her group. She had a little bedsitter which she said was so terrible she couldn't imagine *anyone* wanting to visit it, yet every Friday there was a small drinks party there which people fought to be part of.

Georgia's hair always looked perfect. Compared to all the other girls, who had bad hair days every day, Georgia looked as if she had just left an expensive coiffeur. Which she had, actually. She worked in a posh salon on Fridays, their busy day, and in return got a few tips, a good cut every month and a shampoo and blow dry every week.

She must have worked hard at her studies because she was never seen out on week-nights, but on Friday she played hostess to the college's finest, Saturday lunchtimes she was often seen in a pub on the river surrounded by College Heroes, and she'd have a date at the best restaurants on Saturday night.

It was hard to know whether people *liked* her or not. There was something calculated about her even then. Georgia never giggled or confided: she looked at you in a measured way with her big grey eyes, as if she was taking you in somehow. As though she was evaluating you, wondering was there something she could absorb from you for herself.

That's what I thought, anyway. But then obviously I wouldn't warm to Miss Georgia Hall.

Well, I mean, she took James, my boyfriend.

Of course there are those who could and I'm sure *did* say that he wasn't forced to leave me for her, nobody put a noose around his neck or a gun to his head. James walked very willingly to Georgia's side that autumn.

One week he and I were running around catching falling leaves for good luck and the next he was all dressed to kill in a new jacket, taking her to this expensive Grill place that he and I had never been to and that he had often said was rather pretentious, because we couldn't afford it.

He handled it all very badly. 'I suppose you've heard,' he said awkwardly to me. Of course I had heard. College was like a steamy goldfish bowl, everyone heard everything. But I would not let him have the satisfaction of knowing I had already been told.

'Heard what?' I asked. I was never Oscar material, I shouldn't even try to act.

'I know someone must have told you,' he said. 'I'm seeing Georgia.'

'Of course you see Georgia.' I pretended to be dumb, forcing him to admit what I already knew.

'No, I mean *seeing*. In the sense of . . . going out with,' he said.

'Oh,' I said. It wasn't much of a response after all that manipulation.

'I'm sorry,' James said foolishly.

'Well, if you're sorry you're going out with her – *seeing her* – then why do you do it?' I asked.

'No, I'm not sorry I'm going out with her,' he snapped.

'So what *are* you sorry about?' I asked. It was childish, but then I was very hurt. I was entitled to some bit of revenge.

'I'm sorry for upsetting *you*, Moggie,' he said.

I have to have this stupid name, *Moggie*. It's meant to be a pet name for Margaret. I realised later that I needn't stay stuck with it for life. I could have called myself something like Georgia. But by the time I realised that, it was too late.

'Me? Oh, I'm not upset.'

'You're not?' He looked very relieved. Men are *so* simple at times.

'No, not at all.'

He looked at me as if he had never seen me before.

I wondered what he actually did see. I'm not tall and graceful like Georgia Hall, I'm more dumpy in fact, small and square and solid. My eyes look to me to be too close together. I always imagined it made me appear sinister, a bit like a criminal even, though James had always said that I was silly to run myself down. My hair never looked as if it had *seen* a posh hairdresser even if I did actually take it to one. It looked as if it had a life all of its own and grew in different directions.

Unlike Georgia, I had no elegant clothes: no wispy scarves, no floaty skirts. Just the same jacket for ever and a small variety of skirts and trousers. I was studying boring old economics, not lovely, ethereal art history.

No one in their right minds would blame James for his decision.

'You're amazing, Moggie, quite amazing,' he said admiringly.

And I suppose I was. Amazingly mad.

Georgia was practically purring when I met her next. It was outside the dairy where she was buying cheese for her Friday evening soirée.

'James tells me you've been really super about everything,' she said and she rolled the words around before letting them out. I wanted to lift up a big wooden crate which was near us and break it over her head. I mean, it was a real urge, not just a passing fancy. But I beat it back.

It won't last, this romance, I told myself, and then he'll come back on his knees to his Moggie. And I'll make him sweat a bit before I take him back. I smiled at the thought. 'You look quite nice when you smile, Moggie,' the patronising Queen Georgia said. There was an unspoken second half of the sentence, something like *if only you got your teeth fixed* or maybe *if only you weren't so unacceptably tubby* . . . She just left it hanging in the air, allowing me to fill in the blanks.

She can't win for ever, I told myself and smiled again.

But she did seem to be winning for a long, long time. Naturally she finished with James, who of course came bleating back wondering if his Moggie could have it in her heart to forgive him. But actually I didn't have it in my heart. I didn't want him any more. He was no longer the great James who was going to change the world with me, he was a silly, vain man who liked the way the Prom Princess had smiled at him and brought him, temporarily, to a position of power in her Court.

And we all got on with our lives. I got my degree in economics and joined a research foundation where we did a lot of good work and whether we changed the world or not I don't know, but we certainly dug around and found the facts and the statistics to help others change it. And James joined a rather right-wing firm of lawyers whose chambers handled a lot of corporate clients, the kind of people we once thought were the bad guys.

And Georgia Hall?

Oh, Georgia became famous.

She looked so good she was a natural for television, so they always had her on to talk about this art acquisition, or that discovery, or to sum up what somebody had done for art, and she spoke in a clear, unaffected voice prefacing everything by saying, 'It's only my opinion now,' which covered her if she was wrong about something and heaped great praise on her if she was right.

She helped to compile art books. It *was* suggested once that somebody she was collaborating with was going to sue her for taking the credit and doing none of the work. But that was all hushed up. Or possibly it was just gossip – I wasn't the only flying bird whose wings had been singed by Georgia Hall.

Sometimes I used to tell people I had known her both at school and university. But then I stopped. They always wanted details about her, and I realised how very little any of us had known her at all.

Did she have brothers and sisters? I didn't know. Who were her real friends? Hard to say. People who mattered, possibly. That had always been a theme. Instead of the leading lights of the Debating Society, the Dramatic Society, or the Rugby or the Rowing Club, Georgia's friends were now people in the arts, politicians, captains of industry and even minor royals.

She had long left the little bedsitter behind and I heard or read somewhere that she had a *really elegant* London home. It figured.

She was *really elegant* everywhere: at the races, the opera, the Venice Biennale, some fundraising dinner to keep a work of Art in Britain.

I sound as if I was obsessing about her over the years, as if I watched her sky-rocketing with some bitterness and a beady eye. But that's not true as it happens. I was very busy and had little time to spend thinking about and envying the Girl Most Likely, as she had always been known. I had a life of my own.

The foundation where I worked got a lot of attention in the circles where I would appreciate and care about such attention, and I was headhunted by a small go-ahead agency where we did, though I say it myself, magnificent work on exposing inequalities of opportunity. We dealt with issues of class, education, race, religion, prejudice and ignorance. Soon our work and findings were greatly in demand – from universities, investigative journalists and local councillors to campaigners, churchmen and politicians.

And in the agency I met Bob.

Everything changed after that. He had exactly the same dreams as I did, the same belief that life was short and that whatever good had to be done must be done *now*. Bob was an eager, enthusiastic person who believed that people were basically good and all you had to do was to encourage them.

He seemed to like me a lot. No – stop putting yourself down. He loved me.

Bob loved me.

I used to ask him was there something wrong with his

eyesight when he told me I was beautiful. I didn't expect to be considered beautiful. I expected people to think I was basically all right, and I worked hard and I cared a lot and my heart was in the right place. But *beautiful*? No. That would be pushing things.

Bob would get quite annoyed. 'Margaret, one more word and I swear I'm going to insist you wear a bucket over your head. You have beautiful, velvety-brown, loving eyes – so can you shut up about them?' And I did, because in the great scheme of things the closeness of my eyes was quite a small factor.

And life went on well. My picture was often in the newspaper over various projects and my parents were proud of me. They liked Bob and – after I had glared at them a lot – they stopped asking when were they going to see an engagement ring.

Bob and I lived in a small basement flat very near work. We often had work meetings in our own sitting room, and that was where we thought up a great scheme for the agency which really worked well. It involved architects, planners and builders giving instruction to volunteers about building houses in Africa. We got sponsorship from all kinds of people, and huge cooperation from schools. It really caught peoples' imagination.

And now even the arts world had become interested.

They were going to encourage ethnic design and murals for the projects to make them look less functional; now what we needed was someone who could be the public face of an appeal for sponsorship.

'We really need someone like Georgia Hall,' Bob said. 'If only we knew someone who could put us in contact with her.'

I paused for a moment, before wondering aloud would she even consider doing it.

'She would.' Bob was definite. 'I bet you anything she would.'

All right. So I paused longer than I should have. But then my conscience took over. I must not deprive this campaign of Georgia Hall just because I feared her and resented her and had Definite History with her. No, I must tell Bob that I knew her from way back.

'You never said!' He was astounded.

'You never asked,' I replied dully.

'My life is an open book to you and now it appears you have all these secrets,' he complained. 'Is there anything else you never said? Are you married maybe? Are you a millionaire? Do you deal drugs?'

'OK, Bob, I'll write the letter,' I said.

She replied promptly. Very sorry but too many commitments already . . . desolate to have to refuse . . . very worthy cause . . . wish it well. And a small handwritten PS.

Imagine that being you, Moggie, I didn't recognise the name Margaret, thought it was a different person. But on looking at the pictures I should of course have known it was you . . .

She didn't write that she would have known me anywhere. But she meant it.

A part of me was relieved. Oh, all right, be honest. I was *entirely* relieved that she wasn't going to do it.

Bob was undeterred. 'No worries, I'll persuade her,' he said confidently.

My stomach felt as if there was a lump of lead wedged in it as he set about getting in touch with Georgia Hall. All the skills and determination I had so much admired seemed hateful now as he forced his way into a fifteen-minute meeting with her at a television studio. That was all she could give him, he was told. That's all he would need, Bob said.

And he came back triumphant. She had agreed.

'She's very bright,' he said admiringly. 'Sharp as a tack is Georgia.'

I looked at him wordlessly. The lead in my stomach had gone upwards towards my voice box. I couldn't speak. I wondered what Georgia saw when she looked at my Bob.

He was big and sandy-haired, with freckles on his nose. He had an eager, shambling way of expressing himself. He wore a corduroy jacket and a yellow open-necked shirt. He was so much *not* the kind of person she was always seen with, not suave or smooth or dissembling at all.

But perhaps Bob's transparent goodness was fashionable these days, maybe Georgia – who had always been one to spot a trend – had seen the future. A familiar sense of dread came over me, paralysing rational thought. Was I going to do the same this time? Pretend that it didn't matter, that I didn't care?

Had it worked the last time?

Well, in a way it had: James had come back. But by then I didn't want him back. That would not happen with Bob. James was a student flirtation, Bob was my mature and permanent choice. I didn't need the engagement ring or the semi-detached house that my mother thought were the indications of security. I just wanted his love and shared vision. And now it was all happening again. He had come back saying that Georgia was intelligent – *sharp as a tack*, whatever that meant. It proved conclusively that looks were the only thing that mattered in the end. Why had I been so blind for years?

I went to a hairdresser that day. An expensive place. He was a very pleasant man, the stylist. He told me that he and a few friends were going out as volunteers to build houses in Africa. He had recognised me from an interview in the papers.

I felt better after the cut. I told him that I thought I looked less of a fright than I had done before. He laughed uncertainly as if I had been trying to make a joke. I asked him what he would do if he had my small eyes, and he said that he thought my eyes and my heart were huge and had done a great deal for the world already; and I was so touched that my small eyes actually filled with big tears and he had to give me a tissue.

Bob was meeting Georgia at her house to discuss details of the campaign.

I tried to concentrate on work all day but it was hard. And it was hard even to continue breathing when he called later to say that Georgia was fixing something for them to eat in her house.

When he came home the first thing he did was to admire my hair.

'It's lovely,' he said simply.

Pure guilt, I assumed. But I smiled a feeble smile and listened while he told me how quick she was and how streetwise and a dozen other good things he seemed to have noticed about her.

She was coming to the office next day, she wanted to meet the team, and she would go to Africa next week.

'That will cost a bit, knowing the style she'll be used to,' I said sourly.

'No, she's making a point of paying her own way,' he said. He was under her spell just like all the others. Suddenly I knew why witch doctors existed and still exist in different forms – agony aunts, counsellors, lifestyle gurus. People who will help us to find a stronger spell, better magic to vanquish the rival.

Bob was still talking about her. He seemed to have noticed nothing of her house, only Georgia and every word she said.

'She spoke very well of you,' he said.

How *dare* she talk about me before she replaced me. I found myself contemplating killing her when she came into the office the next day. I might ask her to look out of the window and then elbow her through. Or maybe just push her downstairs. It didn't make me feel any better but it did tire me out and I was asleep in no time.

I dressed in my best outfit next day and put on a serious layer of make-up – but of course you could never second-guess Georgia Hall. She was in blue jeans and a floppy sweater and she had her shiny blonde hair tied back with a rubber band. Her grey eyes were enormous as she listened to everyone on the team describing the work that was being done in an African township.

She appraised me as I came in. I felt like a shabby piece of artwork that she was about to expose as a fake.

'Well, Moggie, what a wonderful place for you to work,' she said.

The others looked at me enviously. They thought she was magical, they hadn't noticed that she left hanging the rest of the sentence which went something like *considering you are so hopeless and dumpy and stupid* . . .

And as I knew she would, she found Bob the most wonderful part of this wonderful place she had come to.

'What a performer!' she said when he had finished speaking about the work that was being done with African communities. 'He should have his own television show,' she purred, 'he's so very powerful.'

I felt dizzy. It would happen in front of my eyes, and I was powerless to prevent it. Bob was not a performer, he believed everything he said. But under her corrupting gaze he would *become* a performer. Everything he had worked for would be thrown away.

17

I didn't kill her. I was just too tired and sad. I suppose I worked on autopilot for the day, which seemed to last for about eighteen months. I thought it would never end. And as I had predicted, Bob took her home to go over all that she had learned so that she would be ready for the interview at the airport as she left the following morning for Africa. I waited for him to telephone me to say that he would be going with her, to *organise* things, to oversee it all. I waited patiently. He wouldn't actually say that he had to go *in order to hold her hand* but that's exactly what it would be.

When the phone rang I was almost ready for it.

But it was Georgia. He had actually asked Georgia Hall to ring me. He couldn't even face telling me himself, he knew how upset I would be, he had asked her to do it.

'Oh, *Moggie*,' she said, her voice silky. 'You are *so* lucky, Moggie, but then I always envied you. Always, from the very start.'

'Yes, I suppose you did.' She clearly expected me to bluster and say *nonsense, Georgia, you were the one we all envied and still do*, so of course I decided to go along with the mad premise that I was the object of admiration.

'You always had everything, parents who cared about you and came to school plays and knew how you were getting on, little brothers who thought you were great. And at university you had marvellous friends, real people, not just *poseurs*. Now you have real work with real values, not just posturing like I have to do.'

So that was the route she was going take. I had always had a charmed life so I should be prepared to give up Bob without a squeak because poor Georgia had nothing.

'So?' My voice was glacial.

'So Bob asked me to call you to say he's on his way home

but he'll stop to get a takeaway. Now that's what I call real devotion.'

She was such an actress, if I hadn't known better I'd have believed her, and thought she truly did envy me, but I knew he would be back shortly with the food and that when we had opened the bottle of wine he would tell me that he needed to go with her.

When he came back he was full of plans for the press conference tomorrow at the airport and how he hoped Georgia wouldn't make it into a three-ring circus.

'Maybe it's just me, maybe I bring out the worst in her, but honestly, she's such hard going isn't she?' he said.

I hadn't an idea what he meant.

'I know we should be sorry for her really,' he argued with himself. 'But it's such a fragile existence, thinking entirely of herself. She has to be centre-stage every step of the way: what people will think of her, what she should wear, how she should sound knowledgeable about tribal art that she doesn't really know inside out. Whether it might mean she will get an Honour and if so would it be an MBE or an OBE? She would drive anyone insane. No wonder you never mentioned her to me.'

He had opened the wine. He had said nothing yet about leaving with her tomorrow. But surely he would, he was only softening me up by telling me how feeble she was. Too feeble to go on her own.

But still he didn't say it, and we finished our food talking on about the media attention she would draw to it all and how tragic it was that we needed gimmicks like this to get good people to do good things.

And then he said, 'In an entire evening of self-absorption and self-pity she said only one thing of any interest. She said she had always envied *you*, that you were very sure about everything – what you wanted to do, that your family and friends would always be there, in your belief that the world could be a better place. She said she had lived by image alone and it wasn't necessarily the right star to follow.'

'She revealed all that about herself? She must really think highly of you!' I was astounded.

'Well, I had her number from the start, of course. I could see it was the most important thing to her. That's how I got her to agree to it in the first place. I told her that her image was slipping, it was too brittle, too uncaring, always being seen at the races, the first nights, the parties. It was time for something more substantial, time she got involved in something – and she bought it.'

He smiled gleefully.

'We'll get more support for the project, more houses built and a higher profile, but, goodness, at what a cost. Come here and give me a hug to cheer me up.'

I hugged him, and over his shoulder I caught my reflection in the mirror. Maybe it was the light, but perhaps I did after all have beautiful, velvety-brown, loving eyes . . .

UNTITLED NOVEL
Tracy Chevalier

CHAPTER ONE

Although she never said so directly, Miss Pelham made it plain that she did not want Jem hanging about in her garden. Whenever it wasn't raining, she liked to take a teacup full of broth – its dull, meaty smell visiting the Kellaways upstairs every morning and evening like a persistent suitor – and sit with it on a little bench that faced sideways halfway along the garden. She would remain there for a good hour in the morning, and in the early evening until it got dark. Jem watched her sometimes from their windows upstairs, or round the side of the privy.

Miss Pelham rarely drank from the cup. When she got up to go inside again she would dump the remains over a grape vine growing up the wall next to the bench. She believed the broth did the plant good. Certainly she hoped it would make the vine grow faster and more robust than her neighbour Mr Blake's. 'He never prunes his vine, and that is a mistake, for all vines need a good pruning or the fruit will be small and sour and no treat to any palate,' Miss Pelham confided early on to Jem's mother, before she

21

discovered that Alice Kellaway was not one for confidences.

Jem had spied on the Blake vine over the fence, but since it was only early April there was little to see. It was a young vine, planted within a year or two, and nothing like the gnarled vines he had known in Dorset. He would have to wait until later in the year to judge which vine grew the best grapes.

He avoided Miss Pelham's broth times, but otherwise Jem went into her garden whenever he could – just after dinner, or if Miss Pelham was out, or when it was raining. He didn't mind the rain, though in London a greasier, sootier rain fell than he was used to. Sometimes he would see Miss Pelham's face appear at the window of what he supposed must be her bedroom (he had only ever been, briefly, in her front room), and she would frown at him when she saw that he'd seen her. The frown and the glass made her look older than she probably was, though Jem was never sure how old any woman other than his mother was. He always expected her to tap on the glass and wave him out of the garden. Instead she would disappear, then reappear five minutes later and repeat the scene, until Jem had at last had his fill of green and put her out of her misery by going back inside.

Sometimes his mother cut short this pantomime by herself appearing in the upper window and tapping to get his attention. Alice Kellaway was fearful of many things about Lambeth, but even more fearful that they might have to leave it if they were thrown out of Miss Pelham's house. She often scolded Jem for going into the garden when he knew she didn't like it.

'But Miss Pelham never said we couldn't go there,' Jem complained.

'Don't do things to make her sorry to let out her rooms

to us,' Alice replied, 'or we'll be out on the street and then where would we go?'

Back to the Piddle Valley, Jem would think but never say, even though he suspected his mother often had the same thought.

This day, a fair one in April 1792, three weeks after the Kellaways had arrived in Lambeth, Jem was in Miss Pelham's garden, not to absorb all of the different colours of green growing there as he normally did, but because he had heard a noise. It was late afternoon, still sunny in the corner of the garden near the house, and Miss Pelham was visiting a friend in Battersea. Jem had been helping his father bring a load of elm upstairs and came down to use the privy when he heard a sound like someone exhaling softly: 'Oh.'

There were many other noises at that moment that this particular sound could have been lost amongst: the new leaves of Miss Pelham's laburnum tree rattling in the breeze; the bellowing of a potato seller out front vying with a man who was crying out, 'You that are able, will you buy a ladle!'; and in the distance, likely coming from Hercules Hall, the sound of a hurdy-gurdy playing 'A Hole to Put Poor Robin In' and stopping when the tune went wrong.

It was the quiet yet commanding quality of the 'Oh' that carried through the clamorous late afternoon to Jem's ears and made him leave the privy to investigate. He was not a particularly curious boy, especially during these past weeks when every sight and sound and smell and taste was so new and outlandish that he stopped wondering at it all and closed his eyes and ears and nose and mouth to so much novelty. But this soft 'Oh' was the sort of sound that he might have sought out back home, burrowing into a hedgerow or creeping through a beech-tree wood to the source of the sound.

He looked first at the windows of Miss Pelham's tidy house. She was not there; nor was his mother or father or Maisie looking out from their rooms on the first or second floors. When he was sure he could do so without being seen, Jem stood up on Miss Pelham's broth bench and peered over the fence.

Apart from a man sitting and cranking his hurdy-gurdy, playing badly, it was quiet in the yard. Maggie was disappointed but not surprised. Acts often rehearsed in the yard of Hercules Hall, especially in good weather. But Mr Astley's show would open in a few days, on the Easter Monday, and everyone, horses included, would be at the Amphitheatre now, working until late to perfect their performances.

Maggie's favourite of all the circus acts were the tumblers when they formed a human pyramid, and of course Master John Astley when he had his horse dance a minuet. Simply to be with, though, she preferred Miss Laura Devine, slack-rope dancer and Scottish beauty. Miss Devine's hair was fashionably dark like Maggie's, but much smoother and shinier, and she had a round white face like a moon that she deliberately turned upwards in a most affecting way. Maggie wanted Miss Devine and John Astley to marry, but as far as she knew they never appeared to notice each other. Besides, Master Astley might be a gentleman but he too had taken turns with the girls in the alcoves on Westminster Bridge. Maggie had seen him there, buttoning his breeches afterwards. The next time he rode in the show he looked just as elegant.

The hurdy-gurdy man began to play 'A Hole to Put Poor

Robin In'. As she sketched squares for hopscotch in the dust, Maggie sang along softly:

> One night as I came from the place
> I spied a fair maid by the way.
> She had rosy cheeks and a dimpled chin
> And a hole to put poor Robin in.

When he stopped for a third time on a duff note, she jeered, 'Ho! Who thinks he'll get a place in Mr Astley's show with that rot gut? Mr Astley only takes real musicians, not rubbish like you!'

'Get away with you, you little cat!' the man returned. 'I'll give you a song to remember!' He made to get to his feet, though with the hurdy-gurdy in his lap he couldn't move fast or far. Maggie left the squares she'd drawn and ran across the yard, laughing. People often came to Hercules Hall to perform for Mr Astley with the hope that he might take them on. He always watched and listened, bless him, then gave each a shilling for their time and said he'd think of them if he needed another tightrope walker or birdsong imitator or one-legged dancing fiddler. Those who tried twice for the free shilling, though, got a boot across the yard. Mr Astley had a prodigious memory and never forgot an act, no matter how bad.

At the other side of the yard a passage led out to the street between the houses that made up Hercules Buildings. Maggie headed for it, then changed her mind, and instead turned and cut across the field towards the back walls of the houses' gardens. These gardens were much longer than those of the houses across the fields in York Place where the Butterfields had rooms. Maggie knew well the gardens and fields surrounding Hercules Hall. She liked to hike herself up and peek over the walls of the gardens, looking for surprises. Dick Butterfield often laughed at his daughter for her curiosity, though he encouraged it as well, and came to expect it. 'It'll be your undoing, Mags, you'll see,' he'd say proudly, then with his next breath demand to hear what she'd seen.

Maggie rarely saw much of interest in the gardens, though she told her father otherwise, careful to preserve her reputation for nosing about and seeing what she ought-n't. Of course, there was plenty to report from the goings-on around Mr Astley's house, but her parents and brother could see much of that for themselves – they had a clear view across the fields of the yard from their window.

Today she was not going to bother looking into the gardens, but then she saw a boy's head rise above a wall between two houses and look down into his neighbour's garden. Maggie quickly calculated: he must be spying on the printer, Mr Blake. She frowned at the boy, for she did-n't recognise him. He looked to be about her age, with a narrow face, small, deep-set eyes, and sandy-brown hair that curled below his ears. He was gazing intently into Mr Blake's garden, as if interested but not surprised by what he saw. He reminded her of a dog looking at a movement in the distance and trying to decide if it was quarry worth running after.

No one could spy on others without Maggie doing so as well, and better if possible. She hurried up to the Blakes' back wall and tried to hoist herself up. It was a little too high, so she looked around for something to stand on. A kitchen garden was being planted in part of the field to supply the Astleys with vegetables. One of his nieces was kneeling at the end of a row, tying a string to a stick to mark the line where she had dropped seeds. Maggie ran over to the edge of the garden, grabbed a barrow full of soil and began trundling it back towards the wall.

'Hey!' the Astley niece called, though typically she did not try to follow Maggie. Maggie was often amazed that such a flamboyant man as Mr Astley could have four such dull nieces. She wondered sometimes if she should offer to switch places, just to liven up his house. But then, he was already surrounded by such lively people in his work; perhaps he preferred to go home to a house of quiet, dull girls who were not always turning back flips and juggling.

She pushed the barrow up to the wall and climbed on to the pile of dirt, sinking deep into it and releasing its moist, manure-and-rotting-vegetable stench. Now she was just able to reach the top of the wall, and she pulled herself up on to her elbows, the moss on the brick scraping a broad brown and green stripe down the front of her dress. By the time she'd found toe holds and steadied herself against the wall, the boy had disappeared. Maggie squinted down the long garden. When she saw Mr Blake and his wife at the far end, she smiled.

Jem dropped back on to Miss Pelham's bench when he heard the girl. Then he jumped off and crept to a part of the garden where he could just see her but easily duck out of sight if she looked at him.

She was a messy, lively girl, with tangled black hair and dark eyes that moved about, as if constantly searching for something and not wanting to miss anything. When she found what she was looking for in the next-door garden, she grinned, a V-shaped smile that cracked the lower part of her face open and made her chin as pointy as a cat's. Jem had seen her once or twice before, crisscrossing the fields behind their house or running up and down the alley that led to the front of Hercules Buildings. He didn't know where she lived. There was a hint of roughness about her, of a life lived outdoors the way tinkers did. Her skin had a dark cast to it, though it may just have been dirt. She moved confidently, but though she called out to people and seemed to know everyone, she ran about on her own.

Jem hesitated. He ought to go inside before she discovered him watching her, but part of him wanted her to see him. Then he heard a tap, and there was his mother at the window, tall and anxious, beckoning to him. Jem turned and saw the girl look up at his mother and stop smiling, then let go of the wall and drop out of sight. Jem sighed and turned to go back inside. When he glanced up again at his mother she was staring into the neighbours' garden before abruptly turning away from the window.

'Madam Misery,' Maggie muttered as she trotted along the back walls, keeping close to them so that the woman wouldn't see her. 'What does she care what I do?' A few houses down there were some stables at the end of the garden, and Maggie squatted there, leaning her back against the wall. It was one of her favourite places to sit because the sun warmed the spot for most of the day, and she could see everything going on at Hercules Hall and in the surrounding fields and yet remain out of the way. Not far from her a spotted grey horse was tethered; it pulled the grass around it and ground it rhythmically between its teeth. Maggie closed her eyes to the sun that cut low across the fields and fell on her face, and breathed in the familiar comforting smell of horses. The hurdy-gurdy man was playing again, another popular song that he managed to ruin. Maggie opened her eyes and gazed across the field. The Astley niece was still in the garden; she didn't seem to have noticed that Maggie had not brought back the barrow. 'Chuckle head,' Maggie murmured.

Four children entered the field from the Bastille Row passage opposite. Maggie knew them well – they lived two doors down from the Butterfields. She didn't call to them or get up. She played with other children sometimes, but most of the children about were younger than Maggie; the older ones were working, as maids or messengers, or sweepers or rubbish sifters or stable boys. From time to time Maggie helped her mother with laundry, but hated the sting of lye and the way her hands grew chapped and cracked. Bet Butterfield had begun to make noises about Maggie working more steadily, which Maggie responded to by staying away from the house as much as possible.

She wondered where the boy was now. Perhaps she should go round to the front of the houses that made up Hercules Buildings and see if she could find him. Either that or she could look for her father.

She decided to do both. The children had found her hopscotch squares in the yard, and she waited until they were engaged in playing, while the Astley niece was hoeing with her back to Maggie, to cross back beside the garden walls. As she turned into the alley leading to Hercules Buildings she heard the hurdy-gurdy man behind her begin to play again and sing:

Near to Temple Bar I met a maiden
She was dressed so fine.
She asked me to go with her
To drink a sloop or two of wine.
Up an alley we did sally –

29

Maggie paused and waggled her bum at the man, then chuckled as she ran up the alley.

Hercules Buildings was made up of a row of twenty-two brick houses, bookended by two pubs, The Pineapple and the Hercules Tavern. Each had three storeys as well as a lower-ground floor, with a window per floor, and a small front garden. The street itself was a busy cut-through taken by residents of Lambeth who wanted to cross Westminster Bridge but did not fancy their chances on the quiet, deserted lanes along the river between Lambeth Palace and the bridge. As Maggie emerged on to it, she slipped between pedestrians and made her way past Mr Blake's, the large star-shaped handle of his printing press visible through the window, to the house next door.

Mr Blake's garden was separated from the street by a low wooden fence in need of paint. The gate sagged, and scraped the ground when it was opened and shut. The garden itself was untended, filled with dead leaves, nettles, and brambles. In contrast, the house the boy lived in boasted a shoulder-high iron fence, painted black, with spikes on top. The ground was covered with raked pebbles, broken by a knee-high box hedge grown in a circle, with a bush severely pruned into a ball in the middle. There was little space for such fussy planting, but it was perhaps less surprising if you knew Miss Pelham. Maggie held on to the iron railings, stuck her head between two, and peered through the front window. Faded yellow curtains were pulled half-shut, a clear indication to Maggie that whoever lived in that room was out. If they were in, the curtains would be either completely open to bring light into the room, or closed, to keep people like Maggie from looking in.

As she stepped back from the fence to look up at the win-

dows above, the front door opened and a girl came out carrying a brush and dustpan. She opened the front gate –
which certainly didn't scrape along the ground – and with
a twist of her wrist emptied the pan full of wood shavings
on to the road. As she did so, she giggled and looked about
her. On spying Maggie, she froze, then giggled again, this
time more uncertainly. She was a few years older than
Maggie, though her face was less knowing.

Country girl, Maggie thought. She would jump as high as
the gate if I even hallooed to her. Just from seeing the girl,
Maggie now knew everything about the boy she'd seen earlier. He and his simple sister and doubtless simple parents
were new arrivals from the countryside, coming to London
for the usual reason: to make a better living here than they
did back where they came from. Indeed, sometimes country people did do better. Other times . . . Maggie smiled at
the girl. What a pity she didn't stay in Herefordshire or
Lincolnshire or wherever she was from – whatever those
places were like. Maggie rarely enough went into London
just across the river, and had never been a night away from
home.

She wasn't a bad-looking girl, this simple sister of the
boy. She was flushed rosy and had wider eyes than her
brother, as well as a thin nose with long nostrils that tended to be rubbed red. She did wear a ridiculous frilly white
cap that she must have fancied would go down well in old
London-town. Maggie smirked.

The girl was clearly agitated by Maggie's staring. 'It is all
right just to throw them in the road, isn't it?' she asked.
'I've seen others throw worse.'

At first Maggie didn't understand. Then she snorted.
'You can throw what you like into the street,' she replied.
'That is, now the kennel runs alongside you can. Used to be

TRACY CHEVALIER

it was in the middle and muck got in the way of the horses. But what are you doing throwing out wood shavings
anyhow? Anyone else'd burn them in the fire.'

'Oh, we've plenty for that – too much, really. That's why
I throw most of what I sweep up away.'

'Don't you sell the extra?'

The girl looked puzzled. 'No.'

'You should be selling that, you should. Plenty could do
with shavings to light their fires with. Make yourself a
shilling or two.' Maggie grasped an iron railing and, bal-
anced on one foot, swung around and back in a semi-cir-
cle. 'Tell you what – I could sell it for you, and give you a
penny out of every shilling.'

The girl looked even more confused, as if Maggie were
talking too fast. 'Don't you know how to sell things?'
Maggie said. 'You know, like that.' She indicated an old
woman walking by who cried out, 'Old iron or broken
glass bottles!' and a young girl going the opposite way with
a basket full of wilting posies she'd picked from the fields
surrounding Lambeth. 'See? Everyone's trading something.'

The girl shook her head, the frills on her cap fluttering
around her face. 'We didn't do that, back home.'

'Where's home, then?'

'The Piddle Valley. Near Dorchester. It were a lovely
place.' The girl smiled at something across the road, as if
she could see Dorset there.

Maggie snorted. 'Piddly-diddly-dee, never heard of it.
Well, you're in London now. Best get used to London ways.
Here we sell things.'

'There were no need to sell wood there,' the girl
explained. 'Everywhere you looked there was wood just
lying about, free for the taking.'

32

'What's your name, then, Miss Piddle?'

'Maisie. Maisie Kellaway.'

The door to the house opened, and the woman who'd earlier tapped on the window at Maggie appeared. Alice Kellaway was very tall, and had the same red-tipped nose as Maisie. Her eyes too were rimmed with red, as if she'd been crying, though nothing of the rest of her indicated she was upset. She did not wear a silly cap like Maisie but had her scrubby brown hair pulled back in a bun that hung low on her long neck and made her face look narrow. She might be pretty if she smiled, Maggie thought, but I doubt she ever does.

Alice Kellaway gave Maggie a suspicious look, the way a chandler would who was sure Maggie had nicked some candles from his shop. Maggie knew such looks well – the slant of her eyes made people not trust her – and stood her ground.

Alice Kellaway turned her red eyes to Maisie. 'You're not to go out of the front gate, Maisie. Haven't I told you several times now? You don't know who you'll run into.'

Maggie let go of the railing and folded her arms over her chest. 'Now, ma'am, no need to be cheeky with me, ma'am. Maisie's perfectly safe with me. Safer than with some.'

Maggie's taunt had an unintended effect. Alice Kellaway fastened her eyes on Maggie and nodded. 'You see, Maisie? Even the locals say there are bad sorts about. Even they are cautious. So must you be, child. Come along.'

'That's not what I meant!' Maggie cried, but Alice Kellaway had already taken Maisie's arm and pulled her inside the gate, clanging the latch behind her decisively. With the gate between them, she seemed to feel safer, for she turned around and addressed Maggie once more. 'You can't be too careful here, even you, girl. I've seen some things, just from the window above.'

'Oh, so have I, so have I,' Maggie agreed. 'London's a wicked place, it is.'

'Even today I saw something in the next-door garden.' Alice Kellaway pursed her thin lips.

'I saw it as well, I did.' Maggie chuckled. 'Oh, but there's much worse than that.'

'What? What have you seen?'

Maggie shrugged, caught out for a moment. She did not know what to tell her. There was one thing, of course, that would clearly shock and delight Alice Kellaway, but Maggie did not want to tell her about that. Or, at least, not in any detail.

'Do you know the little lane across Lambeth Green, what runs from the river through the fields to the Royal Row?'

Maisie and Alice Kellaway looked at her blankly. 'It's not far from here,' Maggie continued, impatient for them to understand where it was. 'Just across there.' She pointed across the road, where fields stretched almost unbroken to the river. Lambeth Palace could be seen in the distance, and beyond that, across the river, Westminster Abbey.

'We would never go down to the river,' Alice Kellaway said.

Maggie sighed, the punch taken out of her tale. 'It's a little lane, very useful as a shortcut. It was called Lovers Lane for a time because –' she stopped as the rest of Alice Kellaway's face turned red and she shook her head vehemently, her eyes darting at Maisie.

'Well, it was called that,' Maggie continued, 'but do you know what it's called now?' She paused. 'Cut-Throat Lane!'

Mother and daughter shuddered and Maggie smiled.

Her smile did not last long. 'That is not such a great thing,' came a voice. 'We have a Dead Cat Lane back in the Valley.' The boy was standing in the doorway. No one had noticed him appear.

Maggie rolled her eyes. 'A dead cat? I suppose you found it, did you?'

The boy nodded.

'That's nothing. I found the dead man!' Maggie announced it triumphantly, but even as she did she felt her stomach tighten and contract, as it had done the moment she found the man, and every time she thought of it afterwards. She wished suddenly that she'd kept quiet. She'd never found it easy to keep thoughts to herself.

She was saved from having to say more by Alice Kellaway, who clutched the gate and cried, 'I knew we should never have come to London!'

'Mamma,' Maisie murmured, as if soothing a child.

Jem let Maisie calm their mother. He had heard often enough over the last month of her worries about Lambeth. She had never betrayed such nerviness in Dorset, and her transformation from capable country-woman to anxious city dweller continued to surprise him. If he paid too much attention to her, he began to feel anxious himself, and so he preferred to watch the girl with the messy hair instead. Regret and terror had flashed across her face as she mentioned the dead man she'd found, and when she then swallowed, he felt sure she was tasting bile. Despite her cockiness, Jem pitied her. After all, it was certainly worse to discover a dead man than a dead cat – though the cat had been his, and he'd been fond of it. It had bothered him that the lane was named after the fate of his cat, but there'd been nothing he could do about it. Villagers called places after concrete things, and that was the most certain thing to have happened in that lane.

'Will you show me your lane sometime?' he said. 'It could come in handy.'

Maggie shrugged. 'If you like.' Though she'd not been back to the lane since, she was secretly pleased he'd asked. 'Can't do it now, though. I'm off to find my pa.'

'I can't either,' Jem said. 'I'm helping my father.' He half-held out a long stick of wood that had been partially turned into a leg of a chair. Maggie had not noticed it before.

'Does your pa make chairs, then?'

Jem nodded.

'It's what brought us here!' Maisie interjected. She was an easily excited girl. 'Pa made Mr Astley's chair!'

'Don't say that man's name!' Alice Kellaway almost spat as she said the words. 'I can't bear it!'

Maggie stared at her. Few people apart from her father and hawkers outside the Royal Circus, Mr Astley's main rivals, had a bad word to say about Mr Astley. He was a big, booming, opinionated man, of course, but he was also generous and good-natured to everyone. If he fought you, he forgot it a moment later. Maggie had taken countless pennies from him, and been allowed in free to see shows with a wave of his liberal hand. He never minded that she was her father's daughter, either.

'What's wrong with Mr Astley, then?' she asked, ready to defend him. Already she had tightened her hands into fists.

Alice Kellaway shook her head, turned on her heel, and pushed past Jem through the door. It seemed to Maggie as if the man's name physically propelled her inside the house.

'He's one of the best men you'll meet in Lambeth!'

Maggie called after her. 'If you can't stomach him you'll be hard-pressed to find anyone else to have a drink with!' But Alice Kellaway had disappeared upstairs.

'Mamma is a little upset that we've come to London,' Maisie explained, 'and she blames Mr Astley for putting it into Pa's head to leave Dorset. They met once, you see, when Mr Astley was touring with his show. Pa saw it in Dorchester, and during the show the chair Mr Astley was using for one of his acts when he sits on it while riding atop two horses – well, the chair broke and Pa fixed it for him right there. They got to talking about wood and furniture – did you know that Mr Astley trained as a cabinet maker? Mr Astley told Pa that if he ever wanted to, he should come to London and Mr Astley would help him to set himself up. So that's what he did.'

Maggie frowned. 'Mr A don't ride any more – he's too fat. His son does the chair trick now. John Astley. He lives just there –' she pointed '– just the other side of Mr Blake. He's the best rider they've got, now. And good-looking.'

Maisie's eyes grew bright. 'Is he?'

Maggie chuckled. 'You've got to get out more, go beyond this gate, have more of a look at your neighbours. But that must have been a long time ago. What took you so long to get to London?'

'I was just a little girl when Pa first met Mr Astley. It took him that long to save up the money we needed and convince Mamma.'

'Don't sound like he convinced her.'

'Come along, Maisie,' Jem interrupted, reluctant to have his family's mistakes made public. 'Pa will need you to sweep the workroom.'

'Can I come and see?' Maggie asked. She never missed an opportunity to nose about in others' houses.

'We're busy,' Jem said at the same time as Maisie cried, 'Of course – come in!'

Maggie ignored the boy and started up the stairs behind Maisie.

'Miss Pelham lives on the ground floor,' Maisie explained as they climbed. 'We're to be very careful to keep the stairs and hallway tidy. Mamma insists. That's why I sweep them twice a day, as we track shavings in and out so much. Mr Astley found us these rooms, you know. He owns all of Hercules Buildings.' She stopped on the stairs and lowered her voice. 'Oh, but we're not to mention him around Mamma.'

'I won't.'

'What's your name? I don't even know your name to introduce you to Pa.'

'Maggie. Maggie Butterfield.'

'Oh, are you a Margaret too?' Maisie overflowed with delight. 'Isn't that funny, Jem? We're both Margarets!'

Jem, who had been coming up the stairs behind them, did not answer. He wondered that one name could include two such different girls. He wondered too how he might protect the one from the other. Maisie was clearly keen that Maggie become friends with her, her enthusiasm blinding her to the younger girl's blatant lack of interest in Maisie herself. Maggie was simply curious, and would go where she could. She may even steal something, Jem thought. I'll have to watch her.

Immediately he felt ashamed of this thought. He was often suspicious of people in Lambeth in a way he'd never been in Dorset …

At the top of the stairs, Maisie turned to the right and opened the door to her father's workshop. 'Pa, we have a visitor,' she called out. 'Another Margaret!'

Maggie followed her into the room with growing reluctance. She had never been announced as a visitor before, and did not like the formality of it. She simply wanted to have a look around, not sit and make polite conversation. She glanced back at Jem. He gazed at her coolly. He would not make this easier for her.

I will make you like me, Maggie thought. I will. It was rare for her to feel such a thing ...

When Maggie and Maisie and Jem entered the room, Thomas Kellaway was standing behind a wooden structure that Maggie would later learn was a lathe, used for making chair legs. It reached his waist, with the chair leg held above it in a clamp at shoulder height. A pole hung over his head, with a cord hanging down attached to a treadle under the lathe; when he trod on it the leg was turned around.

Thomas was a slight man of medium height, with tightly-curled sandy hair cut close to his scalp, reminding Maggie of an Airedale terrier her father once had whose fur had to be clipped short when he brushed up against a newly-tarred boat. He was wearing a white shirt and mustard-coloured breeches, and over that a leather apron covered with scratches. Wood shavings had collected all around his feet. He did not look up immediately the door opened, but remained focused on the piece of wood he was turning. Rather than frowning, as many do when they are concentrating, Thomas Kellaway was smiling a small, almost silly smile.

When at last he did look up, his smile broadened, though Maggie felt he was not sure who or what he was smiling at. His light blue eyes looked in her direction, but his gaze seemed to fall just beyond her, as if something in the hallway behind caught his attention, or as if he were blind and could not see what he was looking at. The lines around his eyes gave him a sad air, even as he smiled.

He let his hands rest on the chair leg. 'What did you say, Maisie?' Maggie knew even before he spoke that he would have a soft voice.

'This is Maggie, Pa. We've just met her, haven't we, Jem? She lives – oh, where do you live, Maggie?'

Maggie shuffled her feet in the wood shavings, embarrassed by the attention. 'Across the field,' she mumbled, 'at Bastille Row.'

'Bastille Row? That's an odd name,' Thomas Kellaway said.

'It's really named York Place, but we call it the Bastille. Mr A –' here she was not meant to mention him, and already she had '– he built the houses last year with money he made off a spectacle he put on of the storming of the Bastille.'

Even as she spoke Maggie was looking around. She'd expected to find a room stacked with wood, but there were only a few planks of ash and elm leaning against the wall, and a small pile in the corner of ends and other bits. There was the lathe, of course, as well as various kinds of saws, knives, and chisels, and a battered bench. But there were no finished chairs – just the seat and back of one, with no legs yet. 'Where's your chairs, then? I thought I was coming to sit on one.'

'Gone to the buyers,' Alice Kellaway replied, appearing suddenly in the doorway behind them. 'We never keep a chair round when she's done. What if there was a fire, or thieves?'

'Now, Alice, we never had thieves nor fire in Dorset,' Thomas Kellaway said. 'What makes you think that will happen here?' The mechanical way he said it made clear he

40

had spoken these words many times before; he was now repeating the argument, not with any expectation that it would change his wife's mind, but for the principle of continuing to say what he felt.

Alice Kellaway responded equally automatically. 'And Lambeth isn't Dorset. 'Tis better to have the money safe in hand than a handful of ashes the morning after.' She looked at her husband, and for a brief moment his eyes met hers, before they slid back to the middle distance …

Jem found his father both admirable and embarrassing. He hated Maggie being in the workshop, even though he wanted her to see the skilful work his father did. 'You'll have to come back another time when a chair is finished,' he said, before realising that though the words were a way to get rid of her, they would also bring her back again.

Maggie smiled and snapped her fingers at her side. 'I have to go and find my pa anyhow,' she said, turning on her heel. 'See you before you see me!' She clattered down the stairs before Alice Kellaway could tell her to step softly so that she wouldn't disturb Miss Pelham. Maisie started after her but Alice took hold of her arm to stop her. 'Go and see she's quiet, Jem!' she called to her son. 'Miss Pelham might be back now.'

Maggie was certainly the kind of girl who would disturb Miss Pelham if she could, and she did – not on the stairs but at the front gate …

As Miss Pelham arrived home, having spent a happy day visiting old Battersea friends, she caught sight of some of the wood shavings Maisie had scattered in the street in front of the house and frowned. These shavings were not as offensive as those that Maisie had dumped into Miss Pelham's carefully tended O-shaped hedge in the front garden. And of course it was better the shavings were in the street than on the stairs. But best of all if there were no shavings at all, because no Kellaways at all. Miss Pelham had often regretted over the past few weeks that she'd been so hard on the family who'd rented the rooms from her before the Kellaways. They'd been noisy of a night and the baby had cried constantly towards the end, but at least they didn't track shavings everywhere. Like now: who was that dark-haired scamp coming out of the house with shavings shedding from the soles of her shoes? She had just the sort of sly look that made Miss Pelham clutch her bag more tightly to her chest. 'Here, girl!' she cried. 'What are you doing, coming out of my house? What have you been stealing?'

Before the girl could reply, two people appeared. The boy, Jem, came out behind the girl. And the door to number thirteen, Hercules Buildings opened and Mr Blake stepped out. Miss Pelham shrank back. Mr Blake had never been anything but civil to her – indeed, he nodded at her now – yet he made her nervous.

'Far as I know, this is Mr Astley's house, not yours,' the girl said. Trust her to be cheeky from the start.

Miss Pelham turned to the boy. It was always easier to chide someone who has already been cowed. 'Jem, what is this girl doing here? She's not a friend of yours, I trust?'

'She's – she's made a delivery.' Even in the Piddle Valley, Jem had not been a good liar. He normally kept his mouth shut, but when he spoke he preferred to tell things as they were, or at least as he saw them. He was also old enough now to know that there might be a difference between those two things.

'What did she deliver?' Miss Pelham asked, pouncing on his discomfort. 'Four-day-old fish? Laundry that's not seen a lick of lye?'

42

'Nails,' Maggie cut in. 'I'll be bringing them by regular, won't I, Jem?' She stepped sideways off Miss Pelham's front path and into her garden, where she followed the tiny hedge around in its pointless circle. As she did so, she snapped her fingers at her side again and pressed the top of the hedge with her other hand.

'Get out of my garden, girl!' Miss Pelham cried. 'Jem, get her out of there!'

Maggie laughed, and began to run around the hedge, faster and faster until suddenly she leapt over it into the middle, where the bush pruned into a ball was waiting patiently for her to destroy it. Maggie danced around the leafy ball, sparring at it with her fists while Miss Pelham cried, 'Oh! Oh!' as if each blow were striking her.

Jem watched Maggie box the bush, the tiny leaves showering to the ground, and found himself smiling. He too had been tempted to kick at the absurd hedge so alien from the country hedgerows he was used to. This ridiculous box hedge, ringing a tiny bush, was so useless that no wonder Maisie had dumped the shavings in it that first time. She had no idea that it was meant to be something lovely.

A tap on the window upstairs brought Jem back from Dorset. His mother was glaring down at him and making shooing motions with her hands.

'Maggie – weren't you going to show me something?' Jem said. 'Your – your father, yes? My pa wanted me to – to agree on the price.'

'Aye, that's it. Come on, then.' Maggie ignored Miss Pelham, who was still shouting and swatting ineffectively at her, and pushed through the ring of hedge without bothering to jump it this time. She left behind a gap of broken branches.

'Oh!' cried Miss Pelham for the tenth time. Maggie ran

past her and Jem and out the gate into the street. 'Come on, Jem, you old slug!' she shouted.

As Jem made to follow he glanced at Mr Blake, who had remained still and quiet, his arms crossed over his chest, while Maggie had had her fun with the hedge. He did not seem particularly perturbed by the noise and drama in Miss Pelham's garden. Indeed, they had all of them forgotten that he was there, or Miss Pelham would not have cried 'Oh!' ten times, Maggie would not have beaten the bush, and Jem – well, perhaps Jem would have done the same. He was a boy who found it hard to do anything other than what he did.

Jem had not seen Mr Blake up close before. He was of medium height, solid, with a flat face, a large, heavy brow, sparse brown hair, and the pale complexion of a man who spends much of his time indoors, though now there was patches of red in his cheeks. He had clear grey eyes that were bright like a bird's, and he was looking at them, but he was not watching them. It was not a look like Jem's father, who seemed to be focused on the middle distance. Rather Mr Blake was looking at them, and at the passers-by in the street, and at Lambeth Palace rising up in the distance, and at the clouds behind it. He was taking in everything, without judgement, where Jem's father took in nothing.

'Hello, Sir,' Jem said. It seemed to him to be the right thing to say.

'Hello, my boy,' Mr Blake replied.

'Hallo, Mr Blake!' Maggie called from the street, not to be outdone by Jem. 'How's your missus, then?'

Her cry revived Miss Pelham, who had sunk into herself in Mr Blake's presence. 'Get out of my sight, girl!' she cried. 'I'll have you whipped! Jem, don't you let her back in here. And see her to the end of the street – I don't trust her for a second. She'll steal the gate if we don't watch her!'

'Yes, Ma'am.' Jem glanced at Mr Blake apologetically, but he had already gone to his gate and swung it open. Jem went to join Maggie and they watched as Mr Blake turned left and walked down Hercules Buildings towards the river.

'Let's follow him,' Maggie said.

'No. Let him be.' Jem was surprised at his own decisiveness about the matter.

'Look at his jaunty step. And did you see the colour in his cheeks? And his hair all mussed? We know what he's been up to!'

Jem would not have characterised Mr Blake's pace as jaunty. Rather he was flatfooted, though not plodding. He walked steadily and deliberately, as if he had a destination in mind rather than merely setting out for a stroll. Jem would like to have followed him, not the way Maggie would do it, as a game and a tease, but respectfully, from a distance.

Miss Pelham and Alice Kellaway were still glaring at the children from their respective positions. 'Come along, then,' Jem said, and began to walk along Hercules Buildings in the opposite direction from Mr Blake.

Maggie trotted after him. 'You're really coming with me?'

'Miss Pelham told me to see you to the end of the street.'

Maggie slowed down. 'And you're going to do what that old stick in a dress wants?'

Jem shrugged. 'She's the housekeeper. We have to keep her happy if we're not to be driven out because of the likes of you hanging about.'

Maggie stopped altogether. 'If you're going to be rude, I don't need your escort to the top of the street. I can see my own way around these streets, thanks kindly, and I can guarantee you I won't be coming back to a house where everyone thinks I'm out to nick their things when they haven't got more than me to take anyhow. What makes you think we're so poor I have to steal?'

Jem stopped too. 'I didn't think that! But I don't go beating an old woman's hedge just to bother her, either.'

Maggie began walking again, so that this time Jem was following her. He trailed along behind, not sure what he was doing.

'I'm going to find Pa,' she said. 'Are you coming with me or are you going back home?'

Jem thought of his anxious mother, of his sister so hopeful, of his father absorbed in his chair, and of Miss Pelham waiting by the stairs to pounce on him. 'I'll come with you,' he said, and hurried to catch up with her so that they were walking side by side at last.

Dick Butterfield could have been in one of several pubs. Most people had one local they favoured, where they sat in the same seat, ordered the same drink, saw the same friends, and said the same things. Some nights they joined drinking clubs or societies, when they were meant to discuss topics of mutual interest and provide support to one another. These nights were not much different from other nights except that the beer was cheaper and the songs even bawdier.

Dick Butterfield was something of a club aficionado. He was constantly joining new ones and dropping old ones – though he never cut himself off from a club completely, and his popularity ensured that whenever he reappeared, a cheer went up and a seat was found for him …

What with the weekly chopping and changing, Dick

Butterfield's club and pub life was so complicated that his family rarely knew where he was of an evening. He normally drank within a half-mile radius from his home, but there were still dozens of pubs to choose from. Maggie and Jem had already called in at the Horse and Groom, the Crown and Cushion, the Canterbury Arms, the Old Dover Castle, and the Red Lion, before they at last found him ensconced in the corner of the loudest pub of the lot, the Artichoke on the Lower Marsh . . .

Although it was only early evening, and presumably many had not yet stopped work for the day (Jem felt a pang of guilt thinking of his father standing at the lathe), the pub was heaving with people. The din was tremendous, though after a time his ears began to pick up the pattern of a song, unfamiliar but clearly a tune.

Maggie plunged through the wall of bodies to the corner where her father sat. Dick Butterfield was a small man, very brown – his eyes, his wiry hair, the undertone of his skin, his clothes. Though there was a web of wrinkles extending from the outer corners of his eyes – the badge of someone who smiles widely and often – and his clothes were old, he had a young, energetic air about him. Even though he was sitting, he moved his arms so much, and turned from side to side so often, that he seemed to be running in his seat.

He pulled his daughter on to his lap, and was singing along with the rest of the pub when Jem finally reached them:

And for which I'm sure she'll go to Hell
For she makes me fuck her in church time!

At the last line, a deafening shout went up that made Jem

cover his ears. It was the loudest noise he had ever heard. Maggie had joined in for that last line, and she grinned at Jem. Jem went bright red. Many a song had been sung at the Fox Inn at Folly, but nothing like that.

After the great shout, the pub was quieter, the way a thunderclap directly overhead clears the worst of a storm.

'What have you been up to, then, Mags?' Dick Butterfield asked his daughter.

'This 'n' that. I was at his house –' she pointed at Jem '– this is Jem, Pa – looking at his pa making chairs. They live at Hercules Buildings – next to Mr Blake.'

'Ah yes, printer Blake. Glad to meet you, Jem. Any friend of Mags' – ' he waved his hand '– you know the saying.'

Jem didn't, but knew enough not to admit it. He was catching on. Eventually he *would* know the saying, and many more besides. For now, though, even his catching on needed speeding up. Like his father, he too had to wake up to his new life. Unlike his father, he knew it.

'Sit yourself down, young Jem. Rest your legs.' Dick Butterfield waved at the other side of the table. There was no stool or bench there. Jem looked around. All of the stools in sight were taken. Dick and Maggie Butterfield were gazing at him with identical, brown-eyed expressions – appraising looks, watching and waiting to see what he would do. Jem considered kneeling at the table, but he knew that was not likely to gain the Butterfields' approval. He would have to search the pub for an empty stool. It was expected of him, a little test of his merit – the first real test of his new London life.

Finding an empty stool in a crowded pub is not such a difficult task. But Jem could not find one. He tried asking for one, but those he asked paid no attention to him. He tried to take one that a man was using as a footrest and got swatted about the head. He asked a barmaid, who jeered at him.

Why are all of these people here, Jem thought as he struggled through the scrums of bodies. How is it they can drink now rather than work? In the Piddle Valley no one went to the Fox until the evening.

At last he went back to the table. An empty stool now sat where Dick Butterfield had indicated, and he and Maggie were grinning at Jem.

'Country boy,' muttered a youth sitting next to them who had watched the whole ordeal, including the barmaid's jeering.

'Shut your bone box, Charlie,' Maggie replied. That was when Jem realised that she had a rascally older brother. Charlie Butterfield was much like his father but minus the charm; better-looking in a rough way, and clever, but restless and callous. He used to twist Chinese burns on Maggie's arms until she had grown old enough to put up a better fight. He stopped the day she kicked him in his twiddle-diddles, as Maggie called them. He still looked for ways to get at her – knocking the legs out from the stool she sat on, upending the salt on her food, stealing her blankets in the night.

Of course Jem knew none of this, but he sensed something about Charlie that made him not look him in the eyes for long.

Dick Butterfield tossed sixpence on to the table. 'Fetch Jem a drink, Charlie,' he commanded.

'I'm not –' Charlie sputtered at the same time as Jem said, 'Oh, I don't –' Both stopped at the stern look on Dick Butterfield's face.

And so Charlie got Jem a mug of beer he didn't want – cheap, watery stuff men back at the Fox would spit on to the floor rather than drink.

Dick Butterfield sat back. 'So what have you got to tell me, Mags? What's the scandal today in dear Lambeth?'

'We saw something in Mr Blake's garden, didn't we, Jem?' Maggie gave Jem a sly look. She did see me, then, he thought. She saw me looking, same as I saw her looking. He turned red again but shrugged.

'That's my girl – always sneaking about, finding out what's what.'

Charlie leaned forward. 'What'd you see, then?'

Maggie leaned forward as well. 'We saw him an' his wife at it!'

Charlie chuckled, but Dick Butterfield seemed unimpressed. 'What, tupping is all? That's nothing you don't see every day you look down an alley. Go outside and you'll see it round the corner now. Eh, Jem? I expect you've seen your share of it, back where you come from, eh, boy?'

Jem gazed into his beer. A fly was struggling on the surface, trying not to drown. 'Seen enough,' he mumbled. Of course he had seen it before. It was not just the animals he lived among that he'd seen at it – dogs and cats, sheep, horses, cows, goats, rabbits, chickens, pheasants, quail, even a pair of hedgehogs – but people tucked away in corners of woods or against hedgerows or even in the middle of meadows when they thought no one would pass through. He had seen his neighbours doing it in a barn, and Sam with his girl up at Nettlecombe Tout. He had seen it enough that he was no longer surprised, though he was still embarrassed. It was not that there was so much to see – mostly just clothes and a persistent movement, sometimes a man's pale buttocks pistoning up and down or a woman's breasts pulling from her chest. It was seeing it when he was not expected to, breaking into the assumed privacy, that made Jem turn away with a red face. He had much the same feeling on the rare occasion when he heard his parents argue – as when he heard his mother tell his father she would not go to London, and mild Thomas Kellaway declared that he would go anyway.

Jem dipped his finger into the beer and let the fly climb on to it and fly away. Charlie watched with astonished disgust; Dick Butterfield simply smiled.

'It weren't just that they were doing it,' Maggie interjected. 'They were – they had – they'd taken off all their clothes, hadn't they, Jem? We could see everything, like they were Adam 'n' Eve.'

'That's not –' Jem began.

'And d'you know what they were doing before they did it?'

Dick Butterfield watched his daughter with the same appraising look he'd given Jem when he tried to find a stool. As easygoing as he appeared – lolling on his stool, buying drinks for people, smiling often and nodding – he demanded a great deal from those he was with.

Maggie sat herself up even straighter, delighted to have her father's attention. She thought quickly of the most outlandish thing two people could do when they were meant to be tupping. 'They were reading to each other!'

Charlie chuckled. 'What, the newspaper?'

'No! From a book. It were poetry,' Maggie announced. Specific details always made stories more believable.

'Poetry, eh?' Dick Butterfield repeated. 'I expect that'll be *Paradise Lost*, if they were playing at Adam and Eve in their garden.'

'Yes, that was it. Parrot Eyes Loss,' Maggie agreed. 'I know I heard those words.'

Dick shot her a look. '*Paradise Lost*, Mags. Get your words right.'

'I didn't hear any of that,' Jem stated. He felt Maggie's sharp kick under the table and stopped.

'Course you didn't. You were too far away. It was me that heard it. I heard it all.'

Jem opened his mouth to say that actually Maggie had been further away from Mr and Mrs Blake than he had, but that they had both been too far away to hear anything, or see very much. But he didn't say this. After all, he was learning. One thing he was learning was that the Butterfields clearly wanted to hear this story, with all of its embroidery. In fact, it was the embroidery they wanted. Who was he to spoil their fun – though he thought of Mr Blake walking away down Hercules Buildings, his hands behind his back, and couldn't reconcile the solid truth of that image with the one Maggie was conjuring up of the Blakes in the garden. He wondered how she could see the one thing and yet manage still to say the other.

Maggie watched Jem struggling across the table, and wished she had not brought him to meet her father. She should have let him go back to his family, or follow Mr Blake towards the river on his own. He did not understand what Dick Butterfield wanted from people, the sort of talk required of those allowed to sit with him in the pub. Dick Butterfield wanted to be informed and entertained at the same time. To do one or the other was all right for a short sit on the stool he kept hooked around his foot under the table, but it did not guarantee a long audience. For an hour of Dick Butterfield's company, more was needed. Dick was always looking for another way to make money – he made his living out of small, dodgy schemes dreamt up from pub talk – and he wanted to carve those laughter lines even deeper into his face. Life was hard, after all, and what made it easier than a little laughter, as well as a little business putting money in his pocket?

Dick Butterfield could see when people were sinking. He didn't hold it against Jem – indeed, the boy's confused innocence made him feel rather tender towards him, and irritated at his own jaded children. He pushed Maggie abruptly from his knee so that she fell to the floor, where she stared up at him with hurt eyes. 'Lord, child, you're getting heavy,' Dick said, jiggling his knee up and down. 'You've sent my leg to sleep. You'll be needing your own stool now you're getting to lady size.'

'Won't nobody give 'er one, though, and I'm not talking 'bout just the stool,' Charlie sneered. 'Not a stool, nor a knock, if that's what she thinks growing up'll get 'er. Chicken-breasted little cow.'

'Leave off her,' Jem said.

All three Butterfields froze and stared at him, Dick and Charlie leaning with their elbows on the table, Maggie still on the floor between them. Then Charlie made a lunge across the table towards Jem, but Dick Butterfield put his arm out across Maggie and stopped him. 'Give Maggie your stool an' get another one,' he said, his approval of Jem's chivalry clear from the nod he gave Jem.

Charlie glared at Jem but stood up, letting the stool fall backwards, and stalked off. Jem didn't dare turn around to watch him but kept his eyes on the table. He took a gulp of beer. He'd defended Maggie as a reflex, the way he would his own sister.

Maggie got up and righted Charlie's stool, then sat on it. There was space now to make a smart remark, but she rewarded Jem by staying silent.

'So, Jem, your father's a chair maker, is he?' Dick Butterfield said, opening the business part of the conversation since it

seemed unlikely that Jem would entertain them further.
'Where does he get his wood?'

'One of the timber yards by Westminster Bridge.'

'Which one? Bet I can get it for him cheaper.'

'Mr Harris'. Mr Astley introduced Pa to him.'

Dick Butterfield winced at Mr Astley's name, and cursed
himself for boasting too soon. Dick Butterfield could bro-
ker good deals most places, but not when Mr Astley had
got in there before him. He and his landlord kept a wide
berth of each other, though there was a grudging respect
on both sides as well. If Dick had been a wealthy circus
owner, or Mr Astley a weasel-faced small-time rogue, they
might have been remarkably similar.

Dick gave his daughter a brief irritated look, which she
immediately understood. She hung her head – she should
have known to mention Mr Astley's connection with the
Kellaways so that her father wouldn't make such a mistake.

Nonetheless, Dick Butterfield could not drop his boast.
Instead he reinforced it, as a challenge to himself. 'I'll bet
you a row of rum toddies I can get you better wood, and
cheaper too. Leave it with me, lad,' he added, as if it were
Jem who'd approached him for advice. 'I'll see what I can
do. What number are you at Hercules Buildings?'

'Twelve.'

'I'll drop in one day, then, and have a word with your pa.
I'm always happy to help out new neighbours.'

Jem slumped over his half-drunk beer, unable to stop
Maggie's father worming his way into their lives. All he
could think to say was, 'It's the first floor, not the ground.'
He would shelter Miss Pelham from Dick Butterfield, if
not his parents.

'All right, boy.' Dick Butterfield saved him from further
powerlessness by adding, 'You'll be expected back home,

now, won't you? They'll be wondering what kept you.'

Jem nodded and got up from the stool. 'Thank you for the beer, sir.'

'Of course, lad.' Dick Butterfield hooked his foot around Jem's stool and dragged it back under the table. Maggie grabbed Jem's beer and took a gulp. 'See you,' she muttered.

On his way out, Jem passed Charlie standing with a crowd of other young men. Charlie glared at him and shoved one of his friends so that he knocked into Jem. The men laughed and Jem hurried out, glad to get away from the Butterfields – though he knew it was only for the moment.

THE INNOCENT
Harlan Coben

PROLOGUE

You never meant to kill him.

Your name is Matt Hunter. You are twenty years old. You grew up in an upper-middle-class suburb in northern New Jersey, not far from Manhattan. You live on the poorer side of town, but it's a pretty wealthy town. Your parents work hard and love you unconditionally. You are a middle child. You have an older brother whom you worship, and a younger sister whom you tolerate.

Like every kid in your town, you grow up worrying about your future and what college you will get into. You work hard enough and get good, if not spectacular, grades. Your average is an A minus. You don't make the top ten percent but you're close. You have decent extracurricular activities, including a stint as treasurer of the school. You are a letterman for both the football and basketball team – good enough to play Division Three but not for a financial scholarship. You are a bit of a wiseass and naturally charming. In terms of popularity, you hover right below the top echelon. When you take your SATs, your high scores surprise your guidance counselor.

You shoot for the Ivy Leagues, but they are just a little out of your reach. Harvard and Yale reject you outright. Penn and Columbia waitlist you. You end up going to Bowdoin, a small elite college in Brunswick, Maine. You love it there. The class sizes are small. You make friends. You don't have a steady girlfriend, but you probably don't want one anyway. In your sophomore year, you start on the varsity football team as a defensive back. You play JV basketball right off the bat, and now that the senior point guard has graduated, you have a serious chance of getting valuable minutes.

It is then, heading back to campus between the first and second semester of your junior year, that you kill someone.

You have a wonderfully hectic holiday break with your family, but basketball practice beckons. You kiss your mother and father goodbye and drive back to campus with your best friend and roommate, Duff. Duff is from Westchester, New York. He is squat with thick legs. He plays right tackle on the football team and sits the bench for basketball. He is the biggest drinker on campus – Duff never loses a chugging contest.

You drive.

Duff wants to stop at UMass in Amherst, Massachusetts, on the way up. A high-school buddy of his is a member of a wild frat there. They are having a huge party.

You're not enthusiastic, but you're no party pooper. You are more comfortable with smaller gatherings where you pretty much know everyone. Bowdoin has about 1,600 students. UMass has nearly 40,000. It is early January and freezing cold. There is snow on the ground. You see your breath as you walk into the frat house.

You and Duff throw your coats on the pile. You will think about that a lot over the years, that casual toss of the coats. If you'd kept the coat on, if you'd left it in the car, if you'd put it anyplace else . . .

But none of that happened.

The party is OK. It is wild, yes, but it feels to you like a forced wild. Duff's friend wants you both to spend the night in his room. You agree. You drink a fair amount – this is a college party, after all – though not nearly as much as Duff. The party winds down. At some point you both go to get your coats. Duff is holding his beer. He picks up his coat and swings it over his shoulder.

That is when some of his beer spills.

Not a lot. Just a splash. But it's enough.

The beer lands on a red Windbreaker. That's one of the things you remember. It was freezing cold outside, in the teens, and yet someone was just wearing a Windbreaker. The other thing you will never shake from your mind is that a Windbreaker is waterproof. The spilled beer, little as it was, would not harm the coat. It would not stain. It could so easily be rinsed away.

But someone yells, 'Hey!'

He, the owner of the red Windbreaker, is a big guy but not huge. Duff shrugs. He does not apologise. The guy, Mr Red Windbreaker, gets in Duff's face. This is a mistake. You know that Duff is a great fighter with a short fuse. Every school has a Duff – the guy you can never imagine losing a fight.

That's the problem, of course. Every school has a Duff. And once in a while your Duff runs into their Duff.

You try to end it right there, try to laugh it off, but you have two serious beer-marinated headcases with reddening faces and tightening fists. A challenge is issued. You don't remember who made it. You all step outside into the frigid night, and you realise that you are in a heap of trouble.

The big guy with the red Windbreaker has friends with him.

Eight or nine of them. You and Duff are alone. You look for Duff's high-school friend – Mark or Mike or something – but he is nowhere to be found.

The fight begins quickly.

Duff lowers his head bull-like and charges Red Windbreaker. Red Windbreaker steps to the side and catches Duff in a headlock. He punches Duff in the nose. Still holding Duff in the headlock, he punches him again. Then again. And again.

Duff's head is down. He is swinging wildly and with no effect. It is somewhere around the seventh or eighth punch that Duff stops swinging. Red Windbreaker's friends start cheering. Duff's arms drop to his sides.

You want to stop it, but you are not sure how. Red Windbreaker is going about his work methodically, taking his time with his punches, using big windups. His buddies are cheering him on now. They ooh and ahh with each splat.

You are terrified.

Your friend is taking a beating, but you are mostly worried about yourself. That shames you. You want to do something, but you are afraid, seriously afraid. You can't move. Your legs feel like rubber. Your arms tingle. And you hate yourself for that.

Red Windbreaker throws another punch straight into Duff's face. He releases the headlock. Duff drops to the ground like a bag of laundry. Red Windbreaker kicks Duff in the ribs.

You are the worst sort of friend. You are too scared to

help. You will never forget that feeling. Cowardice. It is worse than a beating, you think. Your silence. This awful feeling of dishonor.

Another kick. Duff grunts and rolls on to his back. His face is streaked with crimson red. You will learn later that his injuries were minor. Duff will have two black eyes and numerous bruises. That will be about it. But right now he looks bad. You know that he would never stand by and let you take a beating like this.

You can stand it no longer.

You jump out of the crowd.

All heads turn toward you. For a moment nobody moves. Nobody speaks. Red Windbreaker is breathing hard. You see his breath in the cold. You are shaking. You try to sound rational. Hey, you say, he's had enough. You spread your arms. You try the charming smile. He's lost the fight, you say. It's over. You've won, you tell Red Windbreaker.

Someone jumps you from behind. Arms snake around you, wrapping you in a bear hug.

You are trapped.

Red Windbreaker comes at you now. Your heart is beating against your chest like a bird in too small a cage. You reel your head back. Your skull crashes into someone's nose. Red Windbreaker is closer now. You duck out of the way. Someone else comes out of the crowd. He has blond hair, his complexion ruddy. You figure that he is another one of Red Windbreaker's pals.

His name is Stephen McGrath.

He reaches for you. You buck away like a fish on a hook. More are coming at you. You panic. Stephen McGrath puts his hands on your shoulders. You try to break free. You spin frantically.

That is when you reach out and grab his neck.

Did you lunge at him? Did he pull you or did you push him? You don't know. Did one of you lose your footing on the sidewalk? Was the ice to blame? You will flash back to this moment countless times, but the answer will never be clear.

Either way, you both fall.

Both of your hands are still on his neck. On his throat. You don't let go.

You land with a thud. The back of Stephen McGrath's skull hits the sidewalk curb. There is a sound, an awful hell-spawned crack, something wet and too hollow and unlike anything you have heard before.

The sound marks the end of life as you know it.

You will always remember it. That awful sound. It will never leave you.

Everything stops. You stare down. Stephen McGrath's eyes are open and unblinking. But you know already. You know by the way his body went suddenly slack. You know by that awful hell-spawned crack.

People scatter. You do not move. You do not move for a very long time.

It happens fast then. Campus security arrives. Then the police. You tell them what happened. Your parents hire a hotshot lawyer from New York City. She tells you to plead self-defense. You do.

And you keep hearing that awful sound.

The prosecutor scoffs. Ladies and gentlemen of the jury, he says, the defendant happened to slip with his hands wrapped around Stephen McGrath's throat? Does he really expect us to believe that?

The trial does not go well.

Nothing matters to you. You once cared about grades and playing time. How pathetic. Friends, girls, pecking order, parties, getting ahead, all that stuff. They are vapors.

They have been replaced by the awful sound of that skull cracking against stone.

At the trial, you hear your parents cry, yes, but it is the faces of Sonya and Clark McGrath, the victim's parents, that will haunt you. Sonya McGrath glares at you throughout the proceedings. She dares you to meet her eye.

You can't.

You try to hear the jury announce the verdict, but those other sounds get in the way. The sounds never cease, never let up, even when the judge looks down sternly and sentences you. The press is watching. You will not be sent to a soft white-boy country-club prison. Not now. Not during an election year.

Your mother faints. Your father tries to be strong. Your sister runs out of the courtroom. Your brother, Bernie, stands frozen.

You are put in handcuffs and taken away. Your upbringing does little to prepare you for what lies ahead. You have watched TV and have heard all the tales of prison rape. That does not happen – no sexual assault – but you are beaten with fists during your first week. You make the mistake of identifying who did it. You get beaten twice more and spend three weeks in the infirmary. Years later, you will still sometimes find blood in your urine, a souvenir from a blow to the kidney.

You live in constant fear. When you are let back into the general population, you learn that the only way you can survive is to join a bizarre offshoot of the Aryan Nation. They do not have big ideas or a grandiose vision of what America should be like. They pretty much just love to hate.

Six months into your incarceration your father dies of a heart attack. You know that it's your fault. You want to cry, but you can't.

You spend four years in prison. Four years – the same amount of time most students spend in college. You are just shy of your twenty-fifth birthday. They say you've changed, but you're not really sure.

When you walk out, you step tentatively. As if the ground below your feet might give. As if the earth might simply cave in on you at any time.

In some ways you will always walk like that.

Your brother Bernie is at the gate to meet you. Bernie just got married. His wife, Marsha, is pregnant with their first child. He puts his arms around you. You can almost feel the last four years shed away. Your brother makes a joke. You laugh, really laugh, for the first time in so long.

You were wrong before – your life did not end on that cold night in Amherst. Your brother will help you find normalcy. You will even meet a beautiful woman down the road. Her name is Olivia. She will make you enormously happy.

You will marry her.

One day – nine years after you walk through those gates – you will learn that your beautiful wife is pregnant. You decide to buy camera phones to stay in constant touch. While you're at work, that phone rings.

Your name is Matt Hunter. The phone rings a second time. And then you answer it …

THE ZAHIR
Paulo Coelho

TRANSLATED FROM THE PORTUGUESE
BY MARGARET JULL COSTA

According to the writer Jorge Luis Borges, the idea of the Zahir comes from Islamic tradition and is thought to have arisen at some point in the eighteenth century. *Zahir*, in Arabic, means visible, present, incapable of going unnoticed. It is someone or something which, once we have come into contact with them or it, gradually occupies our every thought, until we can think of nothing else. This can be considered either a state of holiness or of madness.

Faubourg Saint-Pères,
Encyclopaedia of the Fantastic, 1953

Her name is Esther; she is a war correspondent who has just returned from Iraq because of the imminent invasion of that country; she is thirty years old, married, without children. He is an unidentified male, between twenty-three and twenty-five years old, with dark, Mongolian features. The two were last seen in a café in Rue Faubourg St-Honoré.

The police were told that they had met before, although no one knew how often: Esther had always said that the man – who concealed his true identity behind the name Mikhail – was someone very important, although she had never explained whether he was important to her for her career as a journalist or to her as a woman.

The police began a formal investigation. Various theories were put forward – kidnapping, blackmail, a kidnapping that had ended in murder – none of which were beyond the bounds of possibility given that, in her search for information, her work brought her into frequent contact with people who had links with terrorist cells. They discovered that, in the weeks prior to her disappearance, regular sums of money had been withdrawn from her bank account: those in charge of the investigation felt that these could have been payments for information. She had taken no change of clothes with her, but, oddly enough, her passport was nowhere to be found.

He is a stranger, very young, with no police record, with no clue as to his identity.

She is Esther, thirty years old, the winner of two international prizes for journalism, married.

My wife.

I immediately come under suspicion and am detained because I refuse to say where I was on the day she disappeared. However, the prison officer has just opened the door of my cell, saying that I'm a free man.

And why am I a free man? Because nowadays, everyone

knows everything about everyone, you just have to ask and the information is there: where you've used your credit card, where you spend your time, whom you've slept with. In my case, it was even easier: a woman, another journalist, a friend of my wife, and divorced – which is why she doesn't mind revealing she slept with me – came forward as a witness in my favour when she heard that I had been detained. She provided concrete proof that I was with her on the day and the night of Esther's disappearance.

I talk to the chief inspector, who returns my belongings and offers his apologies, adding that my rapid detention was entirely within the law, and that I have no grounds on which to accuse or sue the State. I say that I haven't the slightest intention of doing either of those things, that I am perfectly aware that we are all under constant suspicion and under twenty-four-hour surveillance, even when we have committed no crime.

'You're free to go,' he says, echoing the words of the prison officer.

I ask: Isn't it possible that something really has happened to my wife? She had said to me once that – understandably given her vast network of contacts in the terrorist underworld – she occasionally got the feeling she was being followed.

The inspector changes the subject. I insist, but he says nothing.

I ask if she would be able to travel on her passport, and he says, of course, since she has committed no crime. Why shouldn't she leave and enter the country freely?

'So she may no longer be in France?'

'Do you think she left you because of that woman you've been sleeping with?'

That's none of your business, I reply. The inspector pauses for a second and grows serious; he says that I was arrested as part of routine procedure, but that he is nevertheless very sorry about my wife's disappearance. He is married himself and although he doesn't like my books (so he isn't as ignorant as he looks! He knows who I am!), he can put himself in my shoes and imagine what I must be going through.

I ask him what I should do next. He gives me his card and asks me to get in touch if I hear anything. I've watched this scene in dozens of films, and I'm not convinced; inspectors always know more than they say they do.

He asks me if I have ever met the person who was with Esther the last time she was seen alive. I say that I knew his code name, but didn't know him personally.

He asks if we have any domestic problems. I say that we've been together for ten years and have the same problems most married couples have – nothing more.

He asks, delicately, if we have discussed divorce recently, or if my wife was considering leaving me. I tell him we have never even considered the possibility, and say again that 'like all couples' we have our occasional disagreements.

Frequent or only occasional?

Occasional, I say.

He asks still more delicately if she suspected that I was having an affair with her friend. I tell him that it was the first – and last – time her friend and I had slept together. It wasn't an affair; it came about simply because we had nothing else to do, it had been a bit of a dull day, neither of us had any pressing engagements after lunch, and the game of seduction always adds a little zest to life, which is why we ended up in bed together.

'You go to bed with someone just because it's a bit of a dull day?'

I consider telling him that such matters hardly form part of his investigations, but I need his help, or might need it later on – there is, after all, that invisible institution called the Favour Bank, which I have always found so very useful.

'Sometimes, yes. There's nothing else very interesting to be done, the woman is looking for excitement, I'm looking for adventure, and that's that. The next day, you both pretend that nothing happened, and life goes on.'

He thanks me, holds out his hand and says that in his world, things aren't quite like that. Naturally, boredom and tedium exist, as does the desire to go to bed with someone, but everything is much more controlled, and no one ever acts on their thoughts or desires.

'Perhaps artists have more freedom,' he remarks.

I say that I'm familiar with his world, but have no wish to enter into a comparison between our different views of society and people. I remain silent, awaiting his next move.

'Speaking of freedom,' he says, slightly disappointed at this writer's refusal to enter into a debate with a police officer, 'you're free to go. Now that I've met you, I'll read your books. I know I said I didn't like them, but the truth is I've never actually read them.'

This is not the first or the last time that I will hear these words. At least this whole episode has gained me another reader. I shake his hand and leave.

I'm free. I'm out of prison, my wife has disappeared in mysterious circumstances, I have no fixed timetable for work, I have no problem meeting new people, I'm rich, famous, and if Esther really has left me, I'll soon find someone to replace her. I'm free, independent.

But what is freedom?

I've spent a large part of my life enslaved to one thing or another, so I should know the meaning of the word. Ever since I was a child, I have fought to make freedom my most precious commodity. I fought with my parents, who wanted me to be an engineer, not a writer. I fought with the other boys at school, who immediately honed in on me as the butt of their cruel jokes, and only after much blood had flowed from my nose and from theirs, only after many afternoons when I had to hide my scars from my mother – because it was up to me not her to solve my problems – did I manage to show them that I could take a thrashing without bursting into tears. I fought to get a job to support myself, and went to work as a delivery man for a hardware store, so as to be free from that old line in family black-mail: 'We'll give you money, but you'll have to do this, this and this . . . '

I fought – although without success – for the girl I was in love with when I was an adolescent, and who loved me too; she left me in the end because her parents convinced her that I had no future.

I fought against the hostile world of journalism – my next job – where my first boss kept me hanging around for three whole hours and only deigned to take any notice of me when I started tearing up the book he was reading: he looked at me in surprise and saw that here was someone capable of persevering and confronting the enemy, essential qualities for a good reporter. I fought for the socialist ideal, went to prison, came out and went on fighting, feeling like a working-class hero – until, that is, I heard the Beatles and decided that rock music was much more fun than Marx. I fought for the love of my first, second and third wives. I fought to find the courage to leave my first, second and third wives, because the love I felt for them hadn't lasted, and I needed to move on, until I found the person who had been put in this world to find me – and she was none of those three.

I fought for the courage to leave my job on the newspaper and launch myself into the adventure of writing a book, knowing full well that no one in my country could make a living as a writer. I gave up after a year, after writing more than a thousand pages – pages of such genius that even I couldn't understand them.

While I was fighting, I heard other people speaking in the name of freedom, and the more they defended this unique right, the more enslaved they seemed to their parents' wishes, to a marriage in which they had promised to stay with the other person 'for the rest of their lives', to the bathroom scales, to their diet, to half-finished projects, to lovers to whom they were incapable of saying 'No' or 'It's over', to weekends when they were obliged to have lunch with people they didn't even like. Slaves to luxury, to the appearance of luxury, to the appearance of the appearance of luxury. Slaves to a life they had not chosen, but which they had decided to live because someone had managed to convince them that it was all for the best. And so their identical days and nights passed, days and nights in which adventure was just a word in a book or an image on the television that was always on, and whenever a door opened, they would say:

'I'm not interested, I'm not in the mood.'

How could they possibly know if they were in the mood or not if they had never tried? But there was no point in asking; the truth was they were afraid of any change that would upset the world they had grown used to.

The inspector says I'm free. I'm free now and I was free in prison too, because freedom continues to be the thing I prize most in the world. Of course, this has led me to drink wines I did not like, to do things I should not have done and which I will not do again, it has left scars on my body and on my soul, it has meant hurting certain people, although I have since asked their forgiveness, when I realised that I could do absolutely anything except force another person to follow me in my madness, in my lust for life. I don't regret the painful times; I bear my scars as if they were medals. I know that freedom has a high price, as high as that of slavery; the only difference is that you pay with pleasure and a smile, even when that smile is dimmed by tears.

I leave the police station, and it's a beautiful day outside, a sunny Sunday which does not reflect my state of mind at all. My lawyer is waiting for me with a few consoling words and a bunch of flowers. He says that he's phoned round all the hospitals and morgues (the kind of thing you do when someone fails to return home), but has not as yet found Esther. He says that he managed to prevent journalists from finding out where I was being held. He says he needs to talk to me in order to draw up a legal strategy that will help me defend myself against any future accusation. I thank him for all his trouble; I know he's not really interested in drawing up a legal strategy, he just doesn't want to leave me alone, because he's not sure how I'll react (Will I get drunk and be arrested again? Will I cause a scandal? Will I try to kill myself?). I tell him I have some important business to sort out and that we both know perfectly well that I have no problem with the law. He insists, but I give him no choice – after all, I'm a free man.

Freedom. The freedom to be wretchedly alone.

I take a taxi to the centre of Paris and ask to be dropped near the Arc de Triomphe. I set off down the Champs-Elysées towards the Hotel Bristol, where Esther and I always used to meet for hot chocolate whenever one of us came back from some trip abroad. It was our coming-home ritual, a plunge back into the love that bound us together, even though life kept sending us off along ever more diverging paths.

I keep walking. People smile, children are pleased to have been given these few hours of spring in the middle of winter, the traffic flows freely, everything seems to be in order – except that none of them knows that I have just lost my wife, they don't even pretend not to know, they don't even care. Don't they realise the pain I'm in? They should all be feeling sad, sympathetic, supportive of a man whose soul is haemorrhaging love as if it were losing blood; but they continue laughing, immersed in their miserable little lives that only happen on weekends.

What a ridiculous thought! Many of the people I pass must also have their souls in tatters, and I have no idea how or why they are suffering.

SLOW MAN
J. M. Coetzee

1.

The blow catches him from the right, sharp and surprising and painful, like a bolt of electricity, lifting him up off the bicycle. *Relax!* he tells himself as he flies through the air (*flies through the air with the greatest of ease!*), and indeed he can feel his limbs go obediently slack. *Like a cat*, he tells himself: *roll, then spring to your feet, ready for what comes next*. The unusual word *limber* or *limbre* is on the horizon too.

That is not quite as it turns out, however. Whether because his legs disobey or because he is for a moment stunned (he hears rather than feels the impact of his skull on the bitumen, distant, wooden, like a mallet-blow), he does not spring to his feet at all, but on the contrary slides metre after metre, on and on, until he is quite lulled by the sliding.

He lies stretched out, at peace. It is a glorious morning. The sun's touch is kind. There are worse things than letting oneself go slack, waiting for one's strength to return. In fact there might be worse things than having a quick nap. He closes his eyes; the world tilts beneath him, rotates; he goes absent.

Once, briefly, he comes back. The body that had flown so lightly through the air has grown ponderous, so ponderous that for the life of him he cannot lift a finger. And there is someone looming over him, cutting off his air, a youngster with wiry hair and spots along his hairline. 'My bicycle,' he says to the boy, enunciating the difficult word syllable by syllable. He wants to ask what has become of his bicycle, whether it is being taken care of, since, as is well known, a bicycle can disappear in a flash; but before those words will come he is gone again.

2.

He is being rocked from side to side, transported. From afar voices reach him, a hubbub rising and falling to a rhythm of its own. What is going on? If he were to open his eyes he would know. But he cannot do that just yet. Something is coming to him. A letter at a time, *clack clack clack*, a message is being typed on a rose-pink screen that trembles like water each time he blinks and is therefore quite likely his own inner eyelid. E-R-T-Y, say the letters, then F-R-I-V-O-L, then a trembling, then E, then Q-W-E-R-T-Y, on and on.

Frivole. Something like panic sweeps over him. He writhes; from the cavern within a groan wells up and bursts from his throat.

'Pain bad?' says a voice. 'Hold still.' The prick of a needle. An instant later the pain is washed away, then the panic, then consciousness itself.

He awakes in a cocoon of dead air. He tries to sit up but cannot; it is as if he were encased in concrete. Around him whiteness unrelieved: white ceiling, white sheets, white light; also a grainy whiteness like old toothpaste in which his mind seems to be coated, so that he cannot think straight and grows quite desperate. 'What is this?' he mouths or perhaps even shouts, meaning *What is this that is being done to me?* or *What is this place where I find myself?* or even *What is this fate that has befallen me?*

From nowhere a young woman in white appears, pauses, regards him watchfully. Out of the muddle in his head he tries to create an interrogative. Too late! With a smile and a reassuring pat on the arm that he seems strangely to hear but not feel, she moves on.

Is it serious?: if there is time for only one question, then that is what the question ought to be, though what the word *serious* might mean he prefers not to dwell on. But even more urgent than the question of seriousness, more urgent than the lurking question of what exactly it was that happened on Magill Road to blast him into this dead place, is the need to find his way home, shut the door behind him, sit down in familiar surroundings, recover himself.

He tries to touch the right leg, the leg that keeps sending obscure signals that it is now the wrong leg, but his hand will not budge, nothing will budge.

My clothes: perhaps that should be the innocuous preparatory question. *Where are my clothes? Where are my clothes, and how serious is my situation?*

The young woman floats back into his field of vision. 'Clothes,' he says, with an immense effort, raising his eyebrows as high as he can to signify urgency.

'No worries,' says the young woman, and blesses him with another of her smiles, her positively angelic smiles. 'Everything is safe, everything is taken care of. The doctor will be with you in a minute.' And indeed before a minute has passed a young man who must be the doctor referred to has materialised at her side and is murmuring in her ear.

'Paul?' says the young doctor. 'Can you hear me? Do I have the name right, Paul Rayment?'

'Yes,' he says carefully.

'Good day, Paul. You will be feeling a little fuzzy right now. That's because you have had a shot of morphine. We will be going into surgery in a short while. You took a whack, I don't know how much you remember, and it has left your leg a bit of a mess. We are going to have a look and see how much of it we can save.'

Again he arches his eyebrows. 'Save?' he tries to say.

'Save your leg,' repeats the doctor. 'We are going to have to amputate, but we will save what we can.'

Something must happen to his face at this point, because the young man does a surprising thing. He reaches out to touch his cheek, and then lets his hand rest there, cradling his old-man's head. It is the kind of thing a woman might do, a woman who loved one. The gesture embarrasses him but he cannot decently pull away.

'Will you trust me in this?' says the doctor.

Dumbly he blinks his eyes.

'Good.' He pauses. 'We don't have a choice, Paul,' he says. 'It is not one of those situations where we have a choice. Do you understand that? Do I have your consent? I am not going to ask you to sign on the dotted line, but do we have your consent to proceed? We will save what we can, but you took quite a blow, there has been a lot of damage, I can't say right now whether we can save the knee, for example. The knee has been pretty thoroughly mashed, and some of the tibia too.'

As if it knows it is being spoken of, as if these terrible words have roused it from its troubled sleep, the right leg sends him a shaft of jagged white pain. He hears his own gasp, and then the thudding of blood in his ears.

'Right,' says the young man, and pats him lightly on the cheek. 'Time to get moving.'

He awakes very much more at ease with himself. His head is clear, he is his old self (*full of beans!* he thinks), though pleasantly drowsy too, he could settle back into a nap at any moment. The leg that took the whack feels enormous, positively elephantine, but there is no pain.

The door opens and a nurse appears, a new, fresh face. 'Feeling better?' she says, and then quickly, 'Don't try to talk yet. Dr Hansen will be along in a while to have a chat. In the meanwhile there is something we need to do. So could I ask you just to relax while ...'

What she needs to do while he relaxes is, it transpires, to insert a catheter. It is a nasty thing to have done to one; he is glad it is a stranger who is doing it. *This is what it leads to!* he berates himself. *This is what it leads to if you let your attention wander for one moment! And the bicycle: what has become of the bicycle? How am I going to do the shopping now? All my fault for taking Magill Road!* And he curses Magill Road, though in fact he has been cycling Magill Road for years without mishap.

What young Dr Hansen has to present to him, when he arrives, is first a quick overview of his case, to *bring him up to speed*, and then more specific news about his leg, some of it good, some not so good.

First, as regards his condition in general, considering what can and does happen to the human body when it is hit by a car going at speed, he can congratulate himself that it is *not serious*. In fact, it is so much the reverse of serious that he can count himself lucky, fortunate, blessed. The crash left him concussed, yes, but he was saved by the helmet he was wearing. Monitoring will continue, but there is no sign of intracranial bleeding. As for motor functions, the preliminary indication is that they are unimpaired. He lost some blood, but that has been replaced. If he is wondering about the stiffness of his jaw, the jaw is not broken, merely bruised. The abrasions on his back and arm look worse than they are, they will heal in a week or two.

Turning to the leg now, the leg that took the blow, he (Dr Hansen) and his colleagues were not, it turned out, able to save the knee. They had a thorough discussion, and the decision was unanimous. The impact – he will show him later on the X-ray – was directly to the knee, and there was an added component of rotation, so the joint was shattered and twisted at the same time. In a younger person they might perhaps have gone for a reconstruction, but a reconstruction of the required order would entail a whole series of operations, one after another, extending over a year, even two years, with a success rate of less than fifty per cent, so all in all, considering his age, it was thought best to take the leg off cleanly above the knee, leaving a good length of bone for a prosthesis. He (Dr Hansen) hopes he (Paul Rayment) will come to accept the wisdom of that decision.

'I am sure you have plenty of questions,' he concludes, 'and I will be happy to try to answer them, but perhaps not now, better in the morning, after you have had some sleep.'

'Prosthesis,' he says, another difficult word, though now that he understands about the jaw that is not broken, merely bruised, he is less embarrassed about difficult words.

'Prosthesis. Artificial limb. Once the surgical wound has healed we will be fitting a prosthesis. Four weeks, maybe even sooner. In no time at all you will be walking again.

Riding your bicycle too, if you like. After some training. Other questions?'

He shakes his head. *Why did you not ask me first?* he wants to say; but if he utters the words he will lose control, he will start shouting.

'Then I'll speak to you in the morning,' says Dr Hansen. 'Chin up!'

That is not all, however. That is not the end of it. First the violation, then consent to the violation. There are papers to sign before he will be left alone, and the papers prove surprisingly difficult.

Family, for instance. Who and where are his family, the papers ask, and how should they be informed? And insurance. Who are his insurers? What cover does his policy provide?

Insurance is no problem. He is insured to the hilt, there is a card in his wallet to prove it, he is nothing if not prudent (*but where is his wallet, where are his clothes?*). Family is a less straightforward matter. Who are his family? What is the right answer? He has a sister. She passed on twelve years ago, but she still lives in him or with him, just as he has a mother who, at the times when she is not in or with him, awaits the angels' clarion from her plot in the cemetery in Ballarat. A father too, doing his waiting farther away, in the cemetery in Pau, from where he rarely pays visits. Are they his family, the three of them? *Those into whose lives you are born do not pass away*, he would like to inform whoever composed the question. *You bear them with you, as you hope to be borne by those who come after you*. But there is no space on the form for extended answers.

What he can be altogether more definite about is that he has neither wife nor offspring. He was married once, certainly;

but the partner in that enterprise is no longer part of him. She has escaped him, wholly escaped. How she managed the trick he has yet to grasp, but it is so: she has escaped into a life of her own. For all practical purposes, therefore, and certainly for the purposes of the form, he is unmarried: unmarried, single, solitary, alone.

Family: *NONE*, he writes in block letters, the nurse overseeing, and draws lines through the other questions, and signs the forms, both of them. 'Date?' he demands of the nurse. 'Second of July,' she says. He writes the date. Motor functions unimpaired.

The pills he accepts are meant to blunt the pain and make him sleep, but he does not sleep. *This* – this strange bed, this bare room, this smell both antiseptic and faintly urinous – this is clearly no dream, it is the real thing, as real as things get. Yet the whole of today, if it is all the same day, if time still means anything, has the feel of a dream. Certainly this *thing*, which now for the first time he inspects under the sheet, this monstrous object swathed in white and attached to his hip, comes straight out of the land of dreams. And what about the other thing, the thing that the young man with the madly flashing glasses spoke of with such enthusiasm – when will that make its appearance? Not in all his days has he seen a naked prosthesis. The picture that comes to mind is of a wooden shaft with a barb at its head like a harpoon and rubber suckers on its three little feet. It is out of Surrealism. It is out of Dali.

He reaches out a hand (the three middle fingers are strapped together, he notices for the first time) and presses the thing in white. It gives back no sensation at all. It is like a block of wood. *Just a dream,* he says to himself, and falls into the deepest sleep.

*

'Today we're going to have you walking,' says young Dr Hansen. 'This afternoon. Not a long walk, just a few steps to give you the feel of it. Elaine and I will be there to lend a hand.' He nods to the nurse. Nurse Elaine. 'Elaine, can you set it up with Orthopaedics?'

'I don't want to walk today,' he says. He is learning to talk through clenched teeth. It is not just that the jaw is bruised, the molars on that side have been loosened too, he cannot chew. 'I don't want to be rushed. I don't want a prosthesis.'

'That's fine,' says Dr Hansen. 'It's not a prosthesis we are talking about anyway, that is still down the line, this is just rehabilitation, the first step in rehabilitation. But we can start tomorrow or the next day. Just so you can see it isn't the end of the world, losing a leg.'

'Let me say it again: *I don't want a prosthesis.*'

Dr Hansen and Nurse Elaine exchange glances.

'If you don't want a prosthesis, what would you prefer?'

'I would prefer to take care of myself.'

'All right, end of subject, we won't rush you into anything, I promise. Now can I talk to you about your leg? Can I tell you about care of the leg?'

Care of my leg? He is smouldering with anger – can they not see it? *You anaesthetised me and hacked off my leg and dropped it in the refuse for someone to collect and toss into the fire. How can you stand there talking about care of my leg?*

'We have brought the remaining muscle over the end of the bone,' Dr Hansen is saying, demonstrating with cupped hands how they did it, 'and sewn it there. Once the wound heals we want that muscle to form a pad over the bone. During the next few days, from the trauma and from the bed rest, there will be a tendency to oedema and swelling. We need to do something about that. There will also be a tendency for the muscle to retract toward the hip, like this.' He stands sideways, pokes out his behind. 'We counteract that by stretching. Stretching is very important. Elaine will show you some stretching exercises and help you if you need help.'

Nurse Elaine nods.

'Who did this to me?' he says. He cannot shout because he cannot open his jaws, but that suits him, suits his teeth-grinding rage. 'Who hit me?' There are tears in his eyes.

The nights are endless. He is too hot, he is too cold; the leg, closed in its swaddling, itches and cannot be reached. If he holds his breath he can hear the ghostly creeping of his assaulted flesh as it tries to knit itself together again. Outside the sealed window a cricket chants to itself. When sleep comes it is sudden and brief, as if gusts of leftover anaesthetic were coming up from his lungs to overwhelm him.

Night or day, time drags. There is a television set facing the bed, but he has no interest in television or in the magazines some kind agency has provided (*Who*. *Vanity Fair*. *Australian Homes and Gardens*). He stares at his watch face, imprinting the position of the hands on his mind. Then he closes his eyes, tries to think of other things – his own breathing, his grandmother sitting at the kitchen table plucking a chicken, bees among the flowers, anything. He opens his eyes. The hands have not stirred. It is as though they have to push their way through glue.

The clock stands still yet time does not. Even as he lies here he can feel time at work on him like a wasting disease, like the quicklime they pour on corpses. Time is gnawing away at him, devouring one by one the cells that make him up. His cells are going out like lights.

The pills he is given every sixth hour wash away the worst of the pain, which is good, and sometimes send him to sleep, which is better; but they also confuse his mind and bring such panic and terror to his dreams that he baulks at taking them. *Pain is nothing*, he tells himself, *just a warning signal from the body to the brain. Pain is no more the real thing than an X-ray photograph is the real thing.* But of course he is wrong. Pain is the real thing, it does not have to press hard to persuade him of that, it does not have to press at all, merely to send a flash or two; after which he quickly settles for the confusion, the bad dreams.

Someone else has been moved into his room, a man older than himself come back from hip surgery. The man lies all day with his eyes shut. Now and again a pair of nurses close the curtains around his bed and, under cover, attend to his body's needs.

Two oldsters; two old fellows in the same boat. The nurses are good, they are kind and cheery, but beneath their brisk efficiency he can detect – he is not wrong, he has seen it too often in the past – a final indifference to their fate, his and his companion's. From young Dr Hansen he feels, beneath the kindly concern, the same indifference. It is as though at some unconscious level these young people who have been assigned to care for them know they have nothing left to give to the tribe and therefore do not count. *So young and yet so heartless!* he cries to himself. *How did I come to fall into their hands? Better for the old to tend the old, the dying the dying! And what folly to be so alone in the world!*

They talk about his future, they nag him to do the exercises that will prepare him for that future, they chivvy him out of bed; but to him there is no future, the door to the future has been closed and locked. If there were a way of putting an end to himself by some purely mental act he would put an end to himself at once, without further ado. His mind is full of stories of people who bring about their own end – who methodically pay bills, write goodbye notes, burn old love letters, label keys, and then, once everything is in order, don their Sunday best and swallow down the pills they have hoarded for the occasion and settle themselves on their neatly made beds and compose their features for oblivion. Heroes all of them, unsung, unlauded. *I am resolved not to be any trouble.* The only matter they cannot take care of is the body they leave behind, the mound of flesh that, after a day or two, will begin to stink. If only it were possible, if only it were permitted, they would take a taxi to the crematorium, set themselves down before the fatal door, swallow their dose, then before consciousness dwindled press the button that will precipitate them into the flames and allow them to emerge on the other side as nothing but a spadeful of ash, almost weightless.

He is convinced that he would put an end to himself if he could, right now. Yet at the same time that he thinks this thought he knows he will do no such thing. It is only the pain, and the dragging, sleepless nights in this hospital, this zone of humiliation with no place to hide from the pitiless gaze of the young, that make him wish for death.

The implications of being single, solitary and alone are brought home to him most pointedly at the end of the second week of his stay in the land of whiteness.

'You don't have family?' says the night nurse, Janet, the one who allows herself banter with him. 'You don't have friends?' She screws up her nose as she speaks, as though it is a joke he is playing on them all.

'I have all the friends I could wish for,' he replies. 'I am not Robinson Crusoe. I just do not want to see any of them.'

'Seeing your friends would make you feel better,' she says. 'Give you a lift. I am sure.'

'I will receive visitors when I feel like it, thank you,' he says.

He is not irascible by nature, but in this place he allows himself spells of peevishness, tetchiness, choler, since that seems to make it easier for his minders to leave him alone. *He's not so bad under the surface*, he imagines Janet protesting to her colleagues. *That old fart!* he imagines her colleagues reply, snorting with derision.

He knows it is expected of him *now that he is improving* to experience gross desires toward these young women, desires which, because male patients, no matter their age, cannot help themselves, will surface at inconvenient times and must be deflected as quickly and decisively as possible.

The truth is that he has no such desires. His heart is as pure as a babe's. It wins him no credit among the nurses, of course, this purity of heart, nor does he expect it to. Being a lecherous old goat is part of the game, a game he is declining to play.

If he refuses to contact friends, it is simply because he does not want to be seen in his new, curtailed, humiliating, and humiliated state. But of course, one way or another, people get to hear of what happened. They send good wishes, they even call in person. On the telephone it is easy enough to make up a story. *It's only a leg,* he says, with a bitterness that he hopes does not come across on the line. *I will be on crutches for a while, then on a prosthesis.* In person the act is more difficult to bring off, since his detestation of the lumpish thing he will henceforth have to lug around with him is all too plainly written on his face.

From the opening of the chapter, from the incident on Magill Road to the present, he has not behaved well, has not risen to the occasion: that much is clear to him. A golden opportunity was presented to him to set an example of how one accepts with good cheer one of the bitterer blows of fate, and he has spurned it. *Who did this to me?*: when he recalls how he shouted at the no doubt perfectly competent though rather ordinary young Dr Hansen, seeming to mean *Who drove into me?* but really meaning *Who had the impudence to cut off my leg?*, he is suffused with shame. He is not the first person in the world to suffer an unpleasant accident, not the first old man to find himself in hospital with well-intentioned but ultimately indifferent young people going through the motions of caring for him. A leg gone: what is losing a leg, in the larger perspective? In the larger perspective, losing a leg is no more than a rehearsal for losing everything. Whom is he going to shout at when that day arrives? Whom is he going to blame?

Margaret McCord pays a visit. The McCords are his oldest friends in Adelaide; Margaret is upset at having heard so late, and full of righteous indignation against whoever did this to him. 'I hope you are going to sue,' she says. 'I have no intention of suing,' he replies. 'Too many openings for comedy. *I want my leg back, failing which* . . . I leave that side of things to the insurance people.' 'You are making a mistake,' she says. 'People who drive recklessly should be taught a lesson. I suppose they will fit you out with a prosthesis. They make such wonderful prostheses nowadays, you will soon be riding your bicycle again.' 'I don't think so,' he replies. 'That part of my life is over.' Margaret shakes her head. 'What a pity!' she says. 'What a pity!'

Sweet of her to say so, he reflects afterwards. *Poor Paul, poor dear, how difficult, what you are having to go through!*: that was what she meant, what she knew he would understand her to mean. *We all have to go through something of this sort*, he would like to remind her, *in the end*.

What surprises him about the whole hospital business is how swiftly concern passes from patching up his leg ('Excellent!' says Dr Hansen, probing the stump with a handsomely manicured finger. 'It is coming together beautifully. You will soon be yourself again.') to the question of how he will (their word) *cope* once he is set loose in the world again.

Indecently early, or so it seems to him, a social worker, Mrs Putts or Putz, is brought into the picture. 'You're still a young man, Mr Rayment, Paul,' she informs him in the cheery manner she must have been taught to employ upon the old. 'You will want to remain independent, and of course that's good, but for quite some time you are going to need nursing, specialised nursing, which we can help to arrange. In the longer term, even once you are mobile, you are going to need someone to be there for you, to give you a hand, to do the shopping and cooking and cleaning and so forth. Is there no one?'

He thinks it over, shakes his head. 'No, there is no one,' he says; by which he means – and believes Mrs Putts understands – that there is no one who will conceive it as his or her Confucian duty to devote himself or herself to caring for his wants, his cooking and cleaning and so forth.

What interests him in the question is what it reveals about his condition as viewed by Mrs Putts, who must have had franker exchanges with the medical people than have yet been afforded him, franker and more down to earth.

From these down to earth exchanges she has evidently concluded that even *in the longer term* he will not get by without being *given a hand*.

In his own vision of the longer term, the vision he has been fashioning in his more equable moments, his crippled self (stark word, but what other is there?) will somehow or other, with the aid of a crutch or some other support, get by in the world, more slowly than before, perhaps, but what do slow and fast matter any more? But that does not appear to be their vision. In their vision, it would seem, he is not the kind of amputee who masters his new, changed circumstances and generally *copes*, but the crepuscular kind, the kind who, in the absence of professional support, will end up in an institution for the aged and infirm.

If Mrs Putts were prepared to be straight with him he would be straight with her. *I have given plenty of thought to coping*, he would tell her. *I made my preparations long ago; even if the worst comes to the very worst, I will be able to take care of myself.* But the rules of the game make it hard for either of them to be straight. If he told Mrs Putts about the cache of Somnex in the cabinet in the bathroom of his flat, for instance, she might feel bound by the rules of the game to consign him to counselling to protect him from himself.

He sighs. 'From your point of view, from a professional point of view, Mrs Putts, Dorianne,' he says, 'what steps would you suggest?'

'You will need to engage a care-giver, that's for sure,' says Mrs Putts, 'preferably a private nurse, someone with experience of frail care. Not that you are frail, of course. But until you are mobile again we would not want to take chances, would we?'

'No, we would not,' he says.

Frail care. Care of the frail. He had never thought of himself as frail until he saw the X-rays. He found it hard to believe that the spider-bones revealed in the plates could keep him upright, that he could totter around without them snapping. The taller the frailer. Too tall for his own good. *I've never operated on such a tall man,* Dr Hansen had said, *with such long legs.* And had then flushed at his gaffe.

'Do you know offhand, Paul,' says Mrs Putts, 'whether your insurance stretches to frail care?'

A nurse, yet another nurse. A woman with a little white cap and sensible shoes bustling about his flat, calling out in jolly tones, *Time for your pills, Mr R!* 'No, I do not think my insurance will run to that,' he replies.

'Well then you'll have to budget for it, won't you?' says Mrs Putts.

THE DIVIDE
Nicholas Evans

CHAPTER ONE

They rose before dawn and stepped out beneath a moon-
less sky aswarm with stars. Their breath made clouds of
the chill air and their boots crunched on the congealed
gravel of the motel parking lot. The old station wagon
was the only car there, its roof and hood veneered with a
dim refracting frost. The boy fixed their skis to the roof
rack while his father stowed their packs then walked
around to remove the newspaper pinned by the wipers to
the windshield. It was stiff with ice and crackled in his
hands as he balled it. Before they climbed into the car
they lingered a moment, just stood there, listening to the
silence and gazing west at the mountains silhouetted by
stars.

The little town had yet to wake and they drove quietly
north along Main Street, past the courthouse and the gas
station and the old movie theater, through pale pools of
light cast by the street lamps, the car's reflection gliding the
darkened windows of the stores. And the sole witness to
their leaving was a grizzled dog who stood watch at the

edge of town, its head lowered, its eyes ghost green in the headlights.

It was the last day of March and a vestige of plowed snow lay gray along the highway's edge. Heading west across the plains the previous afternoon, there had been a first whisper of green among the bleached grass. Before sunset they had strolled out from the motel along a dirt road and heard a meadow lark whistling as if winter had gone for good. But beyond the rolling ranch land the Rocky Mountain Front, a wall of ancient limestone a hundred miles long, was still encrusted with white and the boy's father said they would surely still find good spring snow.

A mile north of town they branched left from the highway on a road that ran twenty more with barely a bend toward the Front. They saw mule deer and coyote and just as the road turned to gravel a great pale-winged owl swerved from the cottonwoods and glided low ahead of them as if piloting the beam of their lights. And all the while the mountain wall loomed larger, a shadowed, prescient blue, until it seemed to open itself and they found themselves traveling a twisting corridor where a creek of snowmelt tumbled through stands of bare aspen and willow with cliffs of pine and rock the color of bone rearing a thousand feet on either side.

The road was steeper now and when it became treacherous with hardpacked snow the boy's father stopped so they could fit the chains. The air when they got out of the car was icy and windless and loud with the rush of the creek. They spread the chains on the snow in front of the rear wheels and his father climbed back into the driver's seat and inched the car forward until the boy called for him to stop. While his father knelt to fasten them, the boy stamped his feet to warm them and blew on his hands.

'Look,' he said.

His father stood and did so, brushing the snow from his hands. Framed in the V of the valley walls, though far beyond, the peak of a vast snow-covered mountain had just been set ablaze by the first rays of the rising sun. Even as they watched, the shadow of night began to drain from its slopes below a deepening band of gold and pink and white.

They parked the car at the trailhead and could see from the untracked snow that no one else had been there. They sat side by side beneath the tailgate and put on their boots.

The owner of the motel had made sandwiches for them and they ate one apiece and drank steaming sweet coffee and watched the shadows around them slowly fill with light. The first few miles would be steep so they fitted skins to their skis for grip. The boy's father checked the bindings and that their avalanche beepers were working and when he was satisfied that all was in order they shouldered their packs and stepped into their skis.

'You lead,' his father said.

The journey they had planned for that day was a loop of some fifteen miles. They had made the same trip two years before and found some of the best skiing either had ever known. The first three hours were the hardest, a long climb through the forest then a perilous zigzag up the north-east side of a ridge. But it was worth it. The ridge's south face was a perfect, treeless shoulder that dropped in three consecutive slopes into the next drainage. If all went well, by the time they reached the top, the sun would just have angled on to it, softening the top half-inch of snow while the base remained frozen and firm.

These backcountry ski trips had become their yearly ritual and the boy now looked forward to them as much as he knew his father did. His snowboarding friends back home in Great Falls thought he was crazy. If you want to ski, they said, why not go someplace where there's a ski lift? And in truth, on their first trip four years ago in the Tetons, he thought they might be right. To a twelve-year-old it had seemed like a lot of effort for precious little fun; too much up and not enough down. At times he had been close to tears. But he kept a brave face and the following year went again.

His father was away from home on business much of the time and there weren't many things they had ever gotten to do together, just the two of them. Sometimes the boy felt they barely knew each other. Neither one was a great talker. But there was something about traveling together through these wild and remote places that seemed to bind them closer than words ever could. And little by little he had come to understand why his father enjoyed the uphill as much as the down. It was a curious formula of physical and mental energy, as if the burning of one fueled the other. The endless rhythmic repetition, sliding one ski past the other, could send you into a sort of trance. And the thrill and sense of achievement when you reached that faraway summit and saw a slope of virgin spring snow reveal itself below could be close to overwhelming.

Perhaps he had come to feel this way simply because each year he had grown stronger. He was taller than his father now and certainly fitter. And though not yet as wise in his mountaincraft, he had probably become the better skier. Perhaps that was why today, for the first time, his father had let him lead.

For the first hour the trail was darkly walled with lodgepole pine and douglas fir as it rose ever higher along the southern side of the winding canyon. Even though they were still in shadow, the climb soon had them sweating and when they paused to gather breath or to drink or to shed another layer of clothing, they could hear the muted roar of the creek far below. Once they heard the crashing of some large creature somewhere in the timber above them.

'What do you think that was?' the boy said.

'Deer. Moose, maybe.'

'Would the bears be waking up yet?'

His father took a drink from his canteen then wiped his mouth with the back of his glove. This was prime grizzly country and they both knew it.

'Guess so. Days have been warm enough this past week.'

An hour later they had stepped out of the trees and into the sunlight and were picking their way across a gully filled with the crazed debris of an avalanche, great lumps of frozen snow and rock and skewered with trees sundered from their roots.

They reached the ridge a little before ten and stood side by side surveying in silence all that unfolded below and around them, mountain and forest quilted with snow and the flaxen plains beyond. The boy felt that if he squinted hard enough he might even defy science and all the world's horizons and see the backs of their own two selves, tiny figures on some distant snowy peak.

The shoulder below them looked as good as they had hoped. The sun was just upon it and it glistened like white velvet strewn with sequins. They took off their skis and unhitched the skins from which they carefully brushed the snow before stowing them in their packs. There was a cold breeze up here and they put on their jackets then sat on a bench of rock and drank coffee and ate the last of the sandwiches while a pair of ravens swirled and called above them against the lazuline sky.

'So what do you think?' his father asked.

'Looks pretty good.'

'I'd say this is about as close to heaven as a man can get.'

As he spoke one of the ravens banked before them, its shadow passing across his face. It landed a few yards from them along the ridge and the boy tossed a crust of bread toward it which made the bird flutter and lift again, but only for a moment. It resettled and with its head cocked inspected the crust then the boy then the crust again. It seemed almost to have summoned the courage to take it when its mate swooped in and snatched it instead. The first bird gave a raucous call and lifted off in pursuit and the boy and his father laughed and watched them tumble and swerve and squawk their way down into the valley.

As with the climb, the boy led the descent. The snow felt as good beneath his skis as it had looked. The sun had melted the surface just enough to give purchase and he quickly found his rhythm. He spread his arms and opened his chest to the slope below as if he would embrace it, savoring the blissful swishing sound of each turn. His father was right. It was as near to heaven as you could get.

At the foot of the first of the three slopes, where the gradient leveled a little, the boy stopped and looked back to admire his tracks. His father was already skiing down beside them, carefully duplicating each curve, keeping close and precisely parallel, until he arrived alongside and the two of them whooped and slapped each other's upheld palms.

'Good tracks!'

'Yours are coming along too.'

His father laughed and said he would ski the next slope first and that when he got to the next level he would take some photographs of the boy's descent. So the boy watched him ski down and waited for the call and when it came he launched himself into the sunlit air, giving it all he had for the camera.

From where they stood next, at the foot of the second slope, they could see all the way down into the drainage, where the sun had yet to seep. They knew from the last time they had skied here that the creek that ran along the bottom was a series of pools and steep waterfalls. It had been warmer then and there had been a lot less snow and, except for some crusted ice at the pool edges, the running water had been exposed. Now however it lay buried beneath all the heaped snow that had funeled into the creek and all they could see were contours and ominous striations.

His father looked at his watch then shielded his eyes to peer at the sun. The boy knew what he was thinking. Half the slope below them was still in shadow. The air down there would be colder and the snow not yet transformed. Maybe they should wait awhile.

'Looks a little icy,' his father said.

'It'll be OK. As I recall, it was you who fell last time.'

His father looked at him over his sunglasses and smiled.

'OK, hotshot. You'd better go first then.'

He handed the boy the camera.

'Make sure you get some good ones.'

'They'll only be as good as your skiing. Wait till I holler.'

He put the camera in his jacket pocket and grinned at his father as he moved off. The snow for the first few hundred feet was still good. But as he came closer to the rim of the sunlight, he felt the surface harden. When he turned there was almost no grip and no swishing sound, only the rasp of ice against the steel edges of his skis. He stopped where the sun met the shadow and looked up the slope where his father stood against the sky.

'How is it?' his father called.

'Kind of skiddy. It's OK.'

'Wait there. I'm coming.'

The boy took off his gloves and pulled the camera from his pocket. He managed to get a couple of shots with the zoom as his father skied down toward him. The third picture he took would later show the exact moment that things began to go wrong. His father was starting a right turn and as he transferred his weight the edge of his left ski failed to bite and slipped sharply downhill. He tried to correct himself but in the process stepped too hard on his uphill ski and it skidded from under him. His body lurched, his arms and ski poles scything the air as he tried to recapture his balance. He was sliding now and had twisted around so that he was facing up the slope. For a moment it looked almost comical, as if he were pretending to ski uphill. Then he jerked and flipped backward and fell with a thump on to his back and at once began to gather speed.

It briefly occurred to the boy that he might try to block his father's slide, or at least check or slow it, by skiing into his path, though even as he thought it, he realised that the impact would surely knock him over and that he too would be carried down the slope. In any case, it was already too late. His father was accelerating so fast there would be no time to reach him. One ski had already come off and was torpedoing away down the mountain and now the other one came off and the boy moved quickly and reached out with a pole, almost losing his balance. He managed to touch the ski but it was going too fast and rocketed past him.

'Stand up!' he yelled. 'Try and stand up!'

It was what his father had once called to him when he

was falling. He hadn't managed to stand and neither could his father now. As he slithered past, face down now and spread-eagled on the ice, his sunglasses scuttling alongside like an inquisitive crab, he shouted something but the boy couldn't make it out. The father's ski poles, one now badly bent, were still looped to his wrists and trailed above him, thrashing and bouncing wildly on the ice. And still he was gaining speed.

The boy began to ski down after him. And though he was shaky with shock and could feel his heart thumping as if it would break loose from its roots, he knew how vital it was not to fall too. He kept telling himself to stay calm and tried to summon all the technique he had ever learned. Trust the downhill ski, even though it slips. Angulate. Chest away from the mountain, not into it. Finish each turn. Angulate, angulate! Look ahead, for Christsake, not down at the ice, not down at your skis.

There was no grip at all now, but after a few first tentative turns he found he could control the slide of his skis and his confidence began to return. Mesmerised, he watched the dark and diminishing figure sliding away into the shadow of the valley. Just before he disappeared from view, his father called out one last time. And the cry was chilling, high-pitched, like an animal frightened for its life.

The boy slithered to a halt. He was breathing hard and his legs were shaking. He knew it was important to remember the exact point at which his father had vanished, though why he had vanished, the boy couldn't yet figure out. Maybe there was some sudden drop you couldn't see from here. He tried to picture the last time they had skied the slope but couldn't recall whether the lower part of the drainage grew steeper or leveled out. And he couldn't help thinking about what might happen when his father hit the bottom. Would the snow heaped in the creek bed cushion his fall or would it be frozen like rock and break every bone in his body? In all his fretting, the boy had already lost the image of where he had last seen his father. In the shadow below everything looked the same. Maybe there were some marks on the ice that might lead him to the place. He took a deep breath and eased himself forward.

On the very first turn his downhill ski slithered badly and he almost fell. His knees were like jelly and the rest of him was locked with tension and it took him some time to trust himself to move again. Then, a few yards down the slope ahead of him, he saw a dark streak maybe six inches long on the ice. In a barely controlled side-slip he made his way toward it.

It was blood. He looked farther down the slope and saw more. There were scuffing marks in the ice too, probably where his father had tried to find grip with the toes of his boots.

Had the boy been able to ski this same slope in good snow, it would have taken him no more than four or five minutes. But on sheet ice with legs atremble, all he could manage was a side-slip so hesitant and fearful that it took the best part of half an hour. So slow was his descent that the sun overtook him and he watched the band of shadow retreat below him and the trail of blood turn vivid on the pristine snow.

Now, in the glare, he could see that the trail disappeared over a sudden rim and that there was something lying there. And drawing closer, he saw his father's sunglasses, perched on the edge of a last steep section of mountain, as if they had stopped to watch the climax of the show. The boy stopped and picked them up. One of the lenses was cracked and an arm was missing. He put them in his pocket.

The slope below him fell sharply some two hundred feet into the valley bottom which even as he watched was filling with sunlight. He peered down, expecting to see the crumpled form of his father. But there was no sign of him nor sound. Just a dazzling white silence.

Even the trail of blood and scuffing seemed to have vanished. There was a sudden rushing of air and the pair of ravens swooped low over his head and down toward the creek, squawking as if they would show him the way. And as the boy watched their shadows cross the creek he saw one of his father's skis and a dark hole in the rumpled blanket of snow.

Five minutes later he was down there. There was a crater, some ten or twelve feet across, its edges jagged where the frozen snow had cracked and given way. He wasn't yet close enough to see into it.

'Dad?'

There was no answer. All he could hear was a faint trickle of water somewhere below him. Cautiously, he maneuvered his skis sideways, testing the snow with each small step, expecting that at any moment it might collapse and swallow him. It seemed firm. Then he remembered his avalanche beeper. This was exactly what the damn things were for. He took off his gloves and unzipped his jacket and pulled the beeper out and started fiddling with it. But his fingers were shaking and his head so racing with panic that he couldn't remember how the damn thing worked.

'Shit! Shit! Shit!'

'Here! I'm here!'

The boy's heart lurched.

'Dad? Are you OK?'

'Yeah. Be careful.'

'I saw blood.'

'I cut my face. I'm OK. Don't come too near the edge.'

But it was already too late. There was a deep cracking sound and the boy felt the snow tilt beneath his skis and in the next instant he was falling. He caught a brief glimpse of his father's bloodied face staring up at him as the lip of the crater crumbled and then saw nothing but the white of the snow cascading with him.

The next thing he knew, his father was hauling him out of the wreckage, asking him if he was hurt. At first the boy didn't know the answer but said he didn't think so. His father grinned.

'Good job, son. You just made us a way out.'

He nodded and the boy turned and saw what he meant. The collapse had created a kind of ramp for them to climb. They sat staring at each other, his father still grinning and dabbing his cheek with a bloody handkerchief. There was a long gash but it didn't look deep and the bleeding had almost stopped. The boy shook his head.

'Didn't think I'd find you alive.'

'Hope you got that picture.'

'Wow, Dad. That was some fall.'

The walls of the hole in which they sat were layered with shelves of bluish white ice, which their two falls had shattered. It was like being in the cross section of some giant frosted wasp nest. The floor felt firm and when the boy brushed away the snow he saw they were on solid ice. His skis had come off when he fell and lay part buried in the snow. He stood and gathered them up. His father slowly stood too, wincing a little as he did so. The sun was just creeping in on them.

'I guess we ought to have a look for my skis,' he said.

His pack was lying on the ice just next to where the boy had brushed away the snow. A shaft of sun was angling on to it. The boy stooped to pick up the pack and as he did so, something caught his eye, a pale shape in the translucent blue of the ice. His father saw him hesitate.

'What is it?'

'Look. Down here.'

They both knelt and peered into the ice.

'Jesus,' his father said quietly.

It was a human hand. The fingers were splayed, the palm upturned. The boy's father hesitated a moment then brushed away a little more snow until they saw the underside of an arm. They looked at each other. Then, without a word they got to work, brushing and scraping and pushing away the snow, creating a window of ice through which, with every stroke of their gloves, they could see more of what lay encased. Tucked beneath the upper arm, half-concealed by a naked shoulder and peering shyly up at them with one blank eye, they now could see a face. From the swirl of hair, captured as if in a photograph, it looked like a young woman. She lay at an angle, her legs askew and slanting away into the darker ice below. She was wearing some kind of crimson top or jacket that was rucked and twisted and seemed to have torn away from her arm and shoulder. The fabric trailed from her as if she had been frozen in the act of shedding it. Her flesh was the color of parchment.

BLOOD AND SCISSORS
Mark Haddon

It began when George was trying on a black suit in Alders the week before Bob Green's funeral.

It was not the prospect of the funeral that had unsettled him. Nor Bob dying. To be honest he had always found Bob's locker-room bonhomie a little trying and he was secretly rather relieved that they would not be playing squash again. Moreover, the manner in which Bob had died was oddly reassuring, a heart attack watching the Boat Race on television two Sundays before. Susan had come back from her sister's and found him lying on his back in the centre of the room, his legs bent and one hand over his eyes, looking so peaceful she thought he was taking a nap.

It would have been painful, obviously. But one could cope with pain. And the endorphins would have kicked in soon enough, followed by that sensation of one's life rushing before one's eyes which George himself had experienced the previous year when he had fallen from a stepladder, broken his elbow on the rockery and passed out, a sensation which he remembered as being not unpleasant (a spectacular bird's-eye view from the top of Hay Bluff had figured prominently for some reason). The same probably went for that tunnel of bright light as the eyes died, given the number of people who heard the angels calling them home and woke to find a junior doctor standing over them with a pair of defibrillators.

Then . . . nothing. It would have been over.

It was too early, of course. Bob was sixty-one. And it was going to be hard for Susan and the boys, even if Susan would blossom now that she was able to finish her own sentences. But all in all it seemed a good way to go.

No. *It was the lesion which had thrown him.*

He had removed his trousers and was putting on the bottom half of the suit when he noticed a small oval of puffed flesh on his hip, darker than the surrounding skin and flaking slightly. His stomach rose and he was forced to swallow some vomit which appeared suddenly at the back of his mouth. He was sweating profusely.

It was cancer.

He hadn't felt like this since John Zinewski's *Fireball* capsized four years ago and he'd found himself trapped underwater with his ankle knotted in a loop of rope. But that had lasted for three, four seconds at most, and this time there was no one around to right the boat.

He would have to kill himself.

It was not a comforting thought but it was something he could do, and this made him feel a little more in control of the situation.

The only question was how.

Jumping from a tall building was a terrifying idea. Easing your centre of gravity out over the edge of the parapet. The possibility that you might change your mind halfway down. And the last thing he needed at this point was more fear.

Hanging needed equipment and he had no gun. He did,

however, have seven elderly Valium in the bathroom cupboard, enough perhaps to give him the courage to crash the car. There was a big stone gateway on the A16 this side of Stamford. He could hit it doing ninety mph with no difficulty whatsoever.

But what if his nerve failed? What if someone pulled out of the drive? What if he killed someone, paralysed himself and died of cancer in a wheelchair in prison?

'Excuse me, Sir. Would you mind accompanying me back into the store?'

A young man of eighteen or so was staring down at him. He had ginger sideburns and a navy blue uniform several sizes too large for him.

George realised that he was crouching on the tiled threshold outside the shop.

'Sir . . . ?'

George got to his feet. 'I'm terribly sorry.'

'Would you mind accompanying me … '

George looked down and saw that he was still wearing the suit trousers with the fly unbuttoned. He buttoned it rapidly. 'Of course.'

He walked back through the doors then made his way between the handbags and the perfumes towards the menswear department with the security guard at his shoulder.

'I seem to have had some kind of turn.'

'You'll have to discuss that with the manager, I'm afraid, Sir.'

The black thoughts which had filled his mind only seconds before seemed to have occurred a very long time ago. True, he felt a little unsure on his feet, the way you did after slicing your thumb with a chisel, but he felt surprisingly good given the circumstances.

The manager of the menswear department was standing bedside a rack of slippers with his hands crossed over his groin. 'Thank you, John.'

The security guard made a little bow, turned on his heels and walked away.

'Now, Mr . . . '

'Bell. George Bell. My apologies. I . . . '

'Perhaps we should have a word in my office.'

A woman appeared carrying George's trousers. 'He left these in the changing room. His wallet's in the pocket.'

George pressed on. 'I appear to have had some kind of blackout. I really didn't mean to cause any trouble.'

How good it was to be talking to other people. Them saying something. Him saying something in return. The steady tick tock of conversation. He could have carried on like this all afternoon.

'Are you all right, Sir?'

The woman cupped a hand beneath his elbow and he slid downwards and sideways on to a chair which felt more solid, more comfortable and more supportive than he remembered any chair ever feeling.

Things became slightly vague for a few minutes.

Then a cup of tea was placed into his hands.

'Thank you'. He sipped. It was not good tea but it was hot, it was in an actual china mug and holding it was comforting.

'Perhaps we should call you a taxi.'

It was probably best, he thought, to buy the suit another day.

*

He decided not to mention the incident to Jean. She would

only want to talk about it and this was not an appealing proposition.

Talking was, in George's opinion, overrated. You could not turn the television on these days without seeing someone discussing their adoption or explaining why they had attacked their husband with a cleaver. Not that he was averse to talking. Talking was one of life's pleasures. And everyone needed to sound off now and then over a pint of Ruddles, about colleagues who didn't shower frequently enough or teenage sons who had returned home drunk in the small hours and thrown up in the dog's basket. But it did not change anything.

The secret of contentment, George felt, lay in ignoring many things completely. How anyone could work in the same office for ten years or bring up children without putting certain thoughts permanently to the back of their mind was beyond him. And as for that last grim lap when you had a catheter and no teeth, memory loss seemed like a godsend.

He told Jean that he had found nothing right in Alders and would try elsewhere on Monday when he would not have to share the town centre with twelve thousand other people. He then went upstairs to the bathroom and stuck a large plaster over the lesion so that it could no longer be seen.

He slept soundly for most of the night and woke abruptly just before six o'clock when Ronald Burrows, his long-dead Geography teacher, pressed a strip of duct tape over his mouth and hammered a hole into his chest with a woodworking tool of a kind George had never seen before. Oddly, it was the smell which upset him most, a smell like the smell of a poorly cleaned public toilet which has recently been used by a very ill person, heady and curried, a smell, worst of all, which seemed to be coming from the puncture wound in his own body.

He fixed his eyes on the tasselled lampshade directly above his head and kept them there, like a man pulled from a river, waiting for his heart to slow down, still not quite able to believe that he was finally on dry land.

After five minutes he got out of bed and went downstairs. He put two slices of bread into the toaster and took down the espresso maker Jamie had given them for Christmas. It was a ridiculous gadget which they kept on the shelf only for diplomatic reasons. But it felt good now, filling the reservoir with water, pouring coffee into the funnel, squeezing the rubber seal into place and screwing the aluminium sections together. Oddly reminiscent of cousin Dougie's steam engine which he had been allowed to play with during the infamous visit to Poole in 1953. And better than sitting watching the trees in the dark garden sway like sea monsters while the kettle boiled.

The blue flame sighed under the metal base. It was like indoor camping. A bit of an adventure.

The toast pinged up.

That was the weekend, of course, when Dougie burned the frog. How strange, looking back, that the course of an entire life should be spelled out so clearly in five minutes during one August afternoon.

He spread butter and marmalade on the toast while the coffee gargled through. He poured the coffee into a mug and took a sip. It was breathtakingly strong. He added milk till it became a dark suede colour then sat down and picked up the RIBA journal which Jamie had left on his last visit.

The Azman Owen house.

Timber shuttering, sliding glass doors, Bauhaus dining

chairs, the single vase of white lilies on the table. Dear God. Sometimes he longed to see a pair of discarded Y-fronts lying around in an architectural photograph.

'High-frequency constant-amplitude electric internal vibrators were specified for the compaction, to minimise blowholes and to produce a uniform compaction effort…'

The house looked like a bunker. What was it about concrete? In two hundred years were people going to be driving under bridges on the M6 marvelling at the gorgeous staining on the buttresses?

He put the magazine down and started the *Times* crossword.

Nanosecond. Byzantium. Bun in the oven. ~~Whimper~~. Quimper.

Jean appeared at seven-thirty wearing her purple bathrobe. 'Trouble sleeping?'

'Woke up at six. Couldn't quite manage to drift off again.'

'I see you used Jamie's thing.'

'It's rather good, actually.'

Though, to be honest, the coffee had given him a hand-tremor and the uncanny sensation that the nightmare had not yet run its course.

'Can I get you anything? Or are you fully toasted?'

'Some apple juice would be good. Thank you.'

Some mornings he would look at her and be mildly repulsed by this plump, ageing woman with the witch hair and the wattles. Then, on mornings like this . . . 'Love' was perhaps the wrong word, though a couple of months back they had surprised themselves by having sex in that hotel in Blakeney.

He put his arm around her hips and she idly stroked his head in the way you might stroke a dog.

There were days when being a dog seemed an enviable thing.

'I forgot to say.' She peeled away. 'Katie rang last night. They're coming over for lunch.'

'They?'

'She and Jacob and Ray.'

Bloody hell. That was all he needed.

Jean bent into the fridge. 'Just try to be civil.'

A LONG WAY DOWN
Nick Hornby

MARTIN

Can I explain why I wanted to jump off the top of a tower block? Of course I can explain why I wanted to jump off the top of a tower block. I'm not a bloody idiot. I can explain it because it wasn't inexplicable: it was a logical decision, the product of proper thought. It wasn't even very serious thought, either. I don't mean it was whimsical – I just mean that it wasn't terribly complicated, or agonised. Put it this way: say you were, I don't know, an assistant bank manager, in Guildford. And you'd been thinking of emigrating, and then you were offered the job of managing a bank in Sydney. Well, even though it's a pretty straightforward decision, you'd still have to think for a bit, wouldn't you? You'd at least have to work out whether you could bear to move, whether you could leave your friends and colleagues behind, whether you could uproot your wife and kids. You might sit down with a bit of paper and draw up a list of pros and cons. You know:

CONS – aged parents, friends, golf club.

PROS – more money, better quality of life (house with

115

pool, barbecue etc.), sea, sunshine, no left-wing councils banning 'Baa-Baa Black Sheep', no EEC directives banning British sausages etc.

It's no contest, is it? The golf club! Give me a break. Obviously your aged parents give you pause for thought, but that's all it is – a pause, and a brief one, too. You'd be on the phone to the travel agents within ten minutes.

Well, that was me. There simply weren't enough regrets, and lots and lots of reasons to jump. The only things in my 'cons' list were the kids, but I couldn't imagine Cindy letting me see them again anyway. I haven't got any aged parents, and I don't play golf. Suicide was my Sydney. And I say that with no offence to the good people of Sydney intended.

MAUREEN

I told him I was going to a New Year's Eve party. I told him in October. I don't know whether people send out invitations to New Year's Eve parties in October or not. Probably not. (How would I know? I haven't been to one since 1984. June and Brian across the road had one, just before they moved. And even then I only nipped in for an hour or so, after he'd gone to sleep.) But I couldn't wait any longer. I'd been thinking about it since May or June, and I was itching to tell him. Stupid, really. He doesn't understand, I'm sure he doesn't. They tell me to keep talking to him, but you can see that nothing goes in. And what a thing to be itching about anyway! But it goes to show what I had to look forward to, doesn't it?

The moment I told him, I wanted to go straight to confession. Well, I'd lied, hadn't I? I'd lied to my own son. Oh, it was only a tiny, silly lie: I'd told him months in advance that I was going to a party, a party I'd made up. I'd made it up properly, too. I told him whose party it was, and why I'd been invited, and why I wanted to go, and who else would be there. (It was Bridgid's party, Bridgid from the Church. And I'd been invited because her sister was coming over from Cork, and her sister had asked after me in a couple of letters. And I wanted to go because Bridgid's sister had taken her mother-in-law to Lourdes, and I wanted to find out all about it, with a view to taking Matty one day.) But confession wasn't possible, because I knew I would have to repeat the sin, the lie, over and over as the year came to an end. Not only to Matty, but to the people at the nursing home, and ... Well, there isn't anyone else, really. Maybe someone at the Church, or someone in a shop. It's almost comical, when you think about it. If you spend day and night looking after a sick child, there's very little room for sin, and I hadn't done anything worth confessing for donkey's years. And I went from that to sinning so terribly that I couldn't even talk to the priest, because I was going to go on sinning and sinning until the day I died, when I would commit the biggest sin of all. (And why is it the biggest sin of all? All your life you're told that you'll be going to this marvellous place when you pass on. And the one thing you can do to get you there a bit quicker is something that stops you getting there at all. Oh, I can see that it's a kind of queue-jumping. But if someone jumps the queue at the post office, people tut. Or sometimes they say, 'Excuse me, I was here first.' They don't say, 'You will be consumed by hellfire for all eternity.' That would be a bit strong.) It didn't stop me from going to the Church, or from taking Mass. But I only kept going because people would think there was something wrong if I stopped.

As we got closer and closer to the date, I kept passing on little tidbits of information that I told him I'd picked up. Every Sunday I pretended as though I'd learned something new, because Sundays were when I saw Bridgid. 'Bridgid says there'll be dancing.' 'Bridgid's worried that not everyone likes wine and beer, so she'll be providing spirits.' 'Bridgid doesn't know how many people will have eaten already.' If Matty had been able to understand anything, he'd have decided that this Bridgid woman was a lunatic, worrying like that about a little get-together. I blushed every time I saw her at the Church. And of course I wanted to know what she actually was doing on New Year's Eve, but I never asked. If she was planning to have a party, she might've felt that she had to invite me.

I'm ashamed, thinking back. Not about the lies – I'm used to lying now. No, I'm ashamed of how pathetic it all was. One Sunday I found myself telling Matty about where Bridgid was going to buy the ham for the sandwiches. But it was on my mind, New Year's Eve, of course it was, and it was a way of talking about it, without actually saying anything. And I suppose I came to believe in the party a little bit myself, in the way that you come to believe the story in a book. Every now and again I imagined what I'd wear, how much I'd drink, what time I'd leave, whether I'd come home in a taxi. That sort of thing. In the end it was as if I'd actually been. Even in my imagination, though, I couldn't see myself talking to anyone at the party. I was always quite happy to leave it.

JESS

I was at a party downstairs in the squat. It was a shit party, full of all these ancient crusties sitting on the floor drinking cider and smoking huge spliffs and listening to weirdo space-out reggae. At midnight, one of them clapped sarcastically, and a couple of others laughed, and that was it – Happy New Year to you too. You could have turned up to that party as the happiest person in London, and you'd still have wanted to jump off the roof by five past twelve. And I wasn't the happiest person in London anyway. Obviously.

I only went because someone at college told me Chas would be there, but he wasn't. I tried his mobile for the one zillionth time, but it wasn't on. When we first split up, he called me a stalker, but that's like an emotive word, 'stalker', isn't it? I don't think you can call it stalking when it's just phone calls and letters and emails and knocking on the door. And I only turned up at his work twice. Three times, if you count his Christmas party, which I don't, because he said he was going to take me to that anyway. Stalking is when you follow them to the shops and on holiday and all that, isn't it? Well, I never went near any shops. And anyway I didn't think it was stalking when someone owed you an explanation. Being owed an explanation is like being owed money, and not just a fiver, either. Five or six hundred quid minimum, more like. If you were owed five or six hundred quid minimum and the person who owed it to you was avoiding you, then you're bound to knock on his door late at night, when you know he's going to be in. People get serious about that sort of money. They call in debt collectors, and break people's legs, but I never went that far. I showed some restraint.

So even though I could see straight away that he wasn't at this party, I stayed for a while. Where else was I going to go? I was feeling sorry for myself. How can you be eighteen and not have anywhere to go on New Year's Eve, apart from some shit party in some shit squat where you don't know anybody? Well, I managed it. I seem to manage it every year. I make friends easily enough, but then I piss them off, I know that much, even if I'm not sure why or how. And so people and parties disappear.

I pissed Jen off, I'm sure of that. She disappeared, like everyone else.

MARTIN

I'd spent the previous couple of months looking up suicide inquests on the internet, just out of curiosity. And nearly every single time, the coroner says the same thing: 'He took his own life while the balance of his mind was disturbed.' And then you read the story about the poor bastard: his wife was sleeping with his best friend, he'd lost his job, his daughter had been killed in a road accident some months before ... Hello, Mr Coroner? Anyone at home? I'm sorry, but there's no disturbed mental balance here, my friend. I'd say he got it just right. Bad thing upon bad thing upon bad thing until you can't take any more, and then it's off to the nearest multi-storey car park in the family hatchback with a length of rubber tubing. Surely that's fair enough? Surely the coroner's inquest should read, 'He took his own life after sober and careful contemplation of the fucking shambles it had become.'?

Not once did I read a newspaper report which convinced me that the deceased was off the old trolley. You know: 'The Manchester United forward, who was engaged to the current Miss Sweden, had recently achieved a unique double: he is the only man ever to have won the FA Cup and an

Oscar for Best Actor in the same year. The rights to his first novel had just been bought for an undisclosed sum by Steven Spielberg. He was found hanging from a beam in his stables by a member of his staff.' Now, I've never seen a coroner's report like that, but if there were cases in which happy, successful, talented people took their own lives, one could safely come to the conclusion that the old balance was indeed wonky. And I'm not saying that being engaged to Miss Sweden, playing for Manchester United and winning Oscars inoculates you against depression – I'm sure it doesn't. I'm just saying that these things help. Look at the statistics. You're more likely to top yourself if you've just gone through a divorce. Or if you're anorexic. Or if you're unemployed. Or if you're a prostitute. Or if you've fought in a war, or if you've been raped, or if you've lost somebody . . . There are lots and lots of factors that push people over the edge; none of these factors are likely to make you feel anything but fucking miserable.

Two years ago Martin Sharp would not have found himself sitting on a tiny concrete ledge in the middle of the night, looking a hundred feet down at a concrete walkway and wondering whether he'd hear the noise that his bones made when they shattered into tiny pieces. But two years ago Martin Sharp was a different person. I still had my job. I still had a wife. I hadn't slept with a fifteen-year-old. I hadn't been to prison. I hadn't had to talk to my young daughters about a front-page tabloid newspaper article, an article headlined with the word SLEAZEBAG! and illustrated with a picture of me lying on the pavement outside a well-known London nightspot. (What would the headline have been if I had gone over? SLEAZY DOES IT! perhaps. Or maybe SHARP END!) There was, it is fair to say, less reason for ledge-sitting before all that happened. So don't tell me that the balance of my mind was disturbed, because it really didn't feel that way. (What does it mean, anyway, that stuff about 'the balance of the mind'? Is it strictly scientific? Does the mind really wobble up and down in the head like some sort of fish-scale, according to how loopy you are?) Wanting to kill myself was an appropriate and reasonable response to a whole series of unfortunate events that had rendered life unliveable. Oh, yes, I know the shrinks would say that they could have helped, but that's half the trouble with this bloody country, isn't it? No one's willing to face their responsibilities. It's always someone else's fault. Boo-hoo-hoo. Well, I happen to be one of those rare individuals who believe that what went on with Mummy and Daddy had nothing to do with me screwing a fifteen-year-old. I happen to believe that I would have slept with her regardless of whether I'd been breast-fed or not, and it was time to face up to what I'd done.

And what I'd done is, I'd pissed my life away. Literally. Well, OK, not *literally* literally. I hadn't, you know, turned my life into urine and stored it in my bladder and so on and so forth. But I felt as if I'd pissed my life away in the same way that you can piss money away. I'd had a life, full of kids and wives and jobs and all the usual stuff, and I'd somehow managed to mislay it. No, you see, that's not right. I knew where my life was, just as you know where money goes when you piss it away. I hadn't mislaid it at all. I'd spent it. I'd spent my kids and my job and my wife on teenage girls and nightclubs: these things all come at a price, and I'd happily paid it, and suddenly my life wasn't there any more. What would I be leaving behind? On New Year's Eve, it felt as though I'd be saying goodbye to a dim form of consciousness and a semi-functioning digestive system – all the indications of a life, certainly, but none of the content. I didn't even feel sad, particularly. I just felt very stupid, and very angry.

I'm not sitting here now because I suddenly saw sense. The reason I'm sitting here now is because that night turned into as much of a mess as everything else. I couldn't even jump off a fucking tower block without fucking it up.

MAUREEN

On New Year's Eve the nursing home sent their ambulance round for him. You had to pay extra for that, but I didn't mind. How could I? In the end, Matty was going to cost them a lot more than they were costing me. I was only paying for a night, and they were going to pay for the rest of his life.

I thought about hiding some of Matty's stuff, in case they thought it was odd, but no one had to know it was his. I could have had loads of kids, as far as they knew, so I left it there. They came around six, and these two young fellas wheeled him out. I couldn't cry when he went, because then the young fellas would know something was wrong; as far as they knew, I was coming to fetch him at eleven the next morning. I just kissed him on the top of his head and told him to be good at the home, and I held it all in until I'd seen them leave. Then I wept and wept, for about an hour. He'd ruined my life, but he was still my son, and I was never going to see him again, and I couldn't even say goodbye properly. I watched the television for a while, and I did have one or two glasses of sherry, because I knew it would be cold out.

I waited at the bus stop for ten minutes, but then I decided to walk. Knowing that you want to die makes you less scared. I wouldn't have dreamed of walking all that way late at night, especially when the streets are full of drunks, but what did it matter now? Although then, of course, I found myself worrying about being attacked but not murdered – left for dead without actually being dying. Because then I'd be taken to hospital, and they'd find out who I was, and they'd find out about Matty, and all those months of planning would have been a complete waste of time, and I'd come out of hospital owing the home thousands of pounds, and where was I going to find that? But no one attacked me. A couple of people wished me a Happy New Year, but that was about all. There isn't so much to be afraid of, out there. I can remember thinking it was a funny time to find that out, on the last night of my life; I'd spent the rest of it being afraid of everything.

I'd never been to Toppers' House before. I'd just been past it on the bus once or twice. I didn't even know for sure that you could get on to the roof any more, but the door was open, and I just walked up the stairs until I couldn't walk any further. I don't know why it didn't occur to me that you couldn't just jump off whenever you felt like it, but the moment I saw it I realised that they wouldn't let you do that. They'd put this wire up, way up high, and there were curved railings with spikes on the top ... well, that's when I began to panic. I'm not tall, and I'm not very strong, and I'm not as young as I was. I couldn't see how I was going to get over the top of it all, and it had to be that night, because of Matty being in the home and everything. And I started to go through all the other options, but none of them were any good. I didn't want to do it in my own front room, where someone I knew would find me. I wanted to be found by a stranger. And I didn't want to jump in front of a train, because I'd seen a programme on the tele-vision about the poor drivers and how suicides upset them. And I didn't have a car, so I couldn't drive off to a quiet spot and breathe in the exhaust fumes . . .

And then I saw Martin, right over the other side of the roof. I hid in the shadows and watched him. I could see he'd done things properly: he'd brought a little stepladder, and some wire cutters, and he'd managed to climb over the top like that. And he was just sitting on the ledge, dangling his feet, looking down, taking nips out of a little hip flask, smoking, thinking, while I waited. And he smoked and he smoked and I waited and waited until in the end I couldn't wait any more. I know it was his stepladder, but I needed it. It wasn't going to be much use to him.

I never tried to push him. I'm not beefy enough to push a grown man off a ledge. And I wouldn't have tried anyway. It wouldn't have been right; it was up to him whether he jumped or not. I just went up to him and put my hand through the wire and tapped him on the shoulder. I only wanted to ask him if he was going to be long.

JESS

Before I got to the squat, I never had any intention of going on to the roof. Honestly. I'd forgotten about the whole Toppers' House thing until I started speaking to this guy. I think he fancied me, which isn't really saying much, seeing as I was about the only female under thirty who could still stand up. He gave me a fag, and he told me his name was Bong, and when I asked him why he was called Bong he said it was because he always smoked his weed out of a bong. And I went, Does that mean everyone else here is called Spliff? But he was just, like, no, that bloke over there is called Mental Mike. And that one over there is called Puddle. And that one over there is Nicky Turd. And so on, until he'd been through everyone in the room he knew.

But the ten minutes I spent talking to Bong made history. Well, not history like 55BC or 1939. Not historical history, unless one of us goes on to invent a time machine or stops Britain from being invaded by Al-Qaida or something. But who knows what would have happened to us if Bong hadn't fancied me? Because before he started chatting me up I was just about to go home, and Maureen and Martin would be dead now, probably, and ... well, everything would have been different.

When Bong had finished going through his list, he looked at me and he went, You're not thinking of going up on the roof, are you? And I thought, not with you, stoner-brain. And he went, because I can see the pain and desperation in your eyes. I was well pissed by that time, so looking back on it, I'm pretty sure that what he could see in my eyes were seven Bacardi Breezers and two cans of Special Brew. I just went, Oh, really? And he went, Yeah, see, I've been put on suicide watch, to look out for people who've only come here because they want to go upstairs. And I was like, What happens upstairs? And he laughed, and went, You're joking, aren't you? This is Toppers' House, man. This is where people kill themselves. And I would never have thought of it if he hadn't said that.

Everything suddenly made sense. Because even though I'd been about to go home, I couldn't imagine what I'd do when I got there, and I couldn't imagine waking up in the morning. I wanted Chas, and he didn't want me, and I suddenly realised that easily the best thing to do was make my life as short as I possibly could. I almost laughed, it was so neat: I wanted to make my life short, and I was at a party in Toppers' House, and the coincidence was too much. It was like a message from God. OK, it was disappointing that all God had to say to me was, like, Jump off a roof, but I didn't blame Him. What else was he supposed to tell me?

I could feel the weight of everything then – the weight of loneliness, of everything that had gone wrong. I felt heroic, going up those last few flights to the top of the building, dragging that weight along with me. Jumping felt like the only way to get rid of it, the only way to make it work for me instead of against me; I felt so heavy that I knew I'd hit the street in no time. I'd beat the world record for falling off a tower block.

IF YOU WERE ME
Marian Keyes

PROLOGUE

There was no return address on the envelope, which was a little weird, because Americans always do that. Already I was slightly uneasy. Even more so when I saw my name and address – it looked like it had been done by someone who'd just learned to write. (Or, more likely, the old writing-with-your-left-hand-to-disguise-your-handwriting trick. Wouldn't it have been easier to just type the damn thing?)

The sensible woman would not have opened it. The sensible women would have thrown it in the bin and walked away from it. But, apart from a short period between the ages of twenty-nine and thirty, when had I ever been sensible? So I opened it. It was a card, a watercolour of a bowl of droopy-looking flowers. And flimsy enough that I could feel something inside. Money, I thought? A cheque? But I was just being sarcastic, even though there was no one there to hear me and, anyway, I was only saying it in my own head. I opened the card and indeed, there was something inside: a photograph. Why was I being sent this? I already had loads of similar ones. Then I saw that I was wrong. It wasn't him at all. And suddenly I understood everything.

CHAPTER ONE

Mum flung open the sitting-room door and announced, 'Morning, Anna, time for your tablets.'

She tried to march briskly, like nurses she'd seen on hospital dramas but there was so much furniture in the room that instead she had to wrestle her way towards me.

When I'd arrived in Ireland seven weeks earlier, I couldn't climb the stairs, because of my dislocated kneecap, so my parents had thoughtfully moved a bed downstairs into the Good Front Room. Make no mistake, I knew what an honour this was: under normal circumstances we were only let into this room at Christmas time. The rest of the year all familial leisure activities – television-watching, chocolate eating, bickering – took place in the converted garage, a cramped little place with the grand title of Television Room. But when Mum and Dad had (very kindly) moved the bed into the GFR there was nowhere for the other furniture – tasselled couches, tasselled armchairs, glass cabinets displaying china of unparalleled hideousness – to go. Other than a small path cleared for me to hobble in and out through, the room now looked like a discount furniture store, the type where millions of couches are squashed in together, so many that you nearly have to climb over them like you're scrambling over boulders along the seafront.

My bed had been thoughtfully placed in the window bay so that I could look out at passing life. Except that I couldn't: there was a net curtain in place that was as immovable as a metal wall. Not *physically* immovable, you understand, but socially immovable: this is Dublin suburbia and brazenly lifting your nets to have a good look at 'passing life' is a social gaffe akin to painting the front of your house Schiaperelli pink when all the others are variations on ivory. Besides there was no passing life to look at. Except . . . actually, through the gauzy barrier I'd begun to notice that most days an elderly woman stopped to let her dog wee at our gatepost – sometimes I thought the dog, a cute little black-and-white terrier, didn't even want to wee, but it was looking as if the woman was insisting.

'Right, Missy.' Mum consulted a sheet of paper, it was a daily hour-by-hour schedule of all the different pills I had to take. It had to be written down because I had so much stuff – antibiotics, anticoagulants, anti-inflammatories, antidepressants, sleeping pills, high-impact vitamins, painkillers which induced a very pleasant floaty feeling and a member of the Valium family which Mum had ferried away to a secret location and which Helen begged her for most mornings.

All the different packets and jars stood on a small elaborately-carved table – several china dogs had been shifted to make way for them and now sat on the floor looking reproachfully at me – and Mum began sorting through them, popping out capsules and shaking pills from bottles.

'OK, Missy.' She'd never called me Missy before all of this. 'Take these.' She tipped a handful of pills into my mouth and passed me a glass of water. She was very kind really, even if I suspected she was acting out a part.

'Dear Jesus,' a voice said. It was my sister Helen, just home from a night's work. She stood in the doorway of the sitting room, looked around scornfully at all the tassels and asked, 'How can you stand it?'

Helen is the youngest of the five of us and she still lives

in the parental home, even though she's twenty-nine. But why would she move out, she often asks, when she's got a rent-free gig, cable telly and a built-in chauffeur (Dad). The food, of course, she admits, is a problem, but there are ways around everything.

'Hi Honey, you're home,' Mum said. 'How was work?'

After several career changes, Helen – and I'm not making this up, I wish I was – is a private investigator. Mind you, it sounds far more dangerous and exciting than it is, she mostly does white collar crime and 'domestics' – where she has to get photographic evidence of men having affairs. I would find it terribly depressing but she says it doesn't bother her because she always knew that men were total scumbags anyway.

She spends a lot of time sitting in wet hedges with a long-range lens trying to get photographic evidence of the adulterers leaving their lovenest. She could stay in her nice, warm, dry car but then she tends to fall asleep and miss her mark.

'Mum, I'm very stressed,' she said. 'Any chance of a Valium?'

'No.'

'My throat is sore. I'm going to bed.'

Helen, on account of all the time she spends in damp hedges, gets a lot of sore throats.

'I'll bring you up some ice cream in a minute, pet. Tell me, I'm dying to know, did you get your mark?' Mum asked.

Mum loves Helen's job, even more than she loves mine and that's saying a lot. (According to almost everyone, I have The Best Job In The World ™.) Occasionally, when Helen is very bored or scared, Mum even goes to work with her. One of their more exciting cases ever was when Helen was hired to find a missing woman. Helen had to go to the woman's apartment and go through her stuff, look-ing for clues (air tickets to Rio etc, as if . . .) and Mum went along because she loves seeing inside other people's houses. She says it's amazing how dirty people's homes are when they're not expecting visitors. This gives her great relief, making it easier to live in her own less-than-pristine crib. However, because her life had begun to resemble, albeit very briefly, a crime drama, Mum got carried away and tried to break down the locked apartment door by running at it with her shoulder – even though, and I can't stress this enough, *Helen had a key*. And Mum *knew* she had it. It had been given to her by the missing woman's sis-ter and all Mum got for her trouble was a badly mashed shoulder.

'It's not like on the telly,' she complained afterwards, kneading the top of her arm.

Then, apparently, earlier this year someone tried to kill Helen. The general consensus was not so much shock that such a dreadful thing would happen, as amazement that it hadn't come to pass much sooner. Of course, it wasn't real-ly an attempt on her life at all. Someone threw a stone through the television-room window during an episode of *EastEnders* – probably just one of the local teenagers expressing his feelings of youthful alienation, but the next thing Mum was on the phone to everyone saying that someone was trying to 'put the frighteners' on Helen, that they 'wanted her off the case'. As 'the case' was a small, office fraud inquiry where an employer had Helen install a hidden camera to see if his employees were nicking printer cartridges, this seemed a little unlikely. But who was I to rain on their parade – and that's exactly what I would have been doing: they're such drama queens they thought this was a little exciting. Except for Dad and that was just because he was the one who had to sweep up all the broken glass and sellotape a plastic bag over the pane until the glazier arrived, approximately six months later. (I suspect Mum and Helen live in a fantasy world, where they think someone's going to come along and write a series of detective novels about them and turn it into a massively successful TV series. In which they will, it goes without saying, play themselves.)

'Yes, I got him,' she sighed. 'I'm off to bed.' Instead she lay down on one of the couches. 'The man spotted me in the hedge, taking his picture.'

Mum's hand went to her mouth.

'Nothing to worry about, we had a little chat. He asked for my phone number.'

'Gobshite,' she added with quite excoriating scorn.

That's the thing about Helen: she's very beautiful. Men, even those she's spying on for their wives, fall for her. Funnily enough, despite me being three years older than her, she and I look extremely similar: we're both small with long dark hair and almost identical heart-shaped faces. Mum sometimes confuses us with each other, especially when she's not wearing her glasses. But, unlike me, Helen's got some magic pull. She operates on an entirely unique frequency, which enslaves men. Perhaps on the same principle of the whistle that only dogs can hear. When men meet the two of us, you can see their confusion. You can actually *see* them thinking, they *look* the same, but this Helen has bewitched me like a drug, whereas that Anna is just so-what . . .

Not that it ever does the men in question any good. Helen boasts that she's never been in love and I believe her. She's unbothered by sentimentality and has contempt for everyone and everything.

Even Luke, Rachel's boyfriend – well, fiancé now. Luke is so dark and sexy and testosteroney that I dread being alone with him. I mean, he's a lovely person, really really lovely, but just, you know . . . all man. I both fancy him and am repelled by him, if that makes any sense and everyone – even Mum – I'd say even *Dad* – is sexually attracted to him. Not Helen though. She reserves particular derision for him and his long dark hair.

All of a sudden Mum seized my arm – luckily, my unbroken one – and hissed, in a voice throbbing with excitement. 'Look! It's Angela Kilfeather. With her girlfriend! She must be home visiting!'

Angela Kilfeather was the most exotic creature that ever came out of our road. Well, that's not really true, my family is far more dramatic what with broken marriages and suicide attempts and drug addiction and Helen, but Mum uses Angela Kilfeather as the gold standard: bad and all as her daughters are, at least they're not lesbians who frenchkiss their girlfriends beside suburban leylandii.

She placed one eye up against the gap between the net curtain and the wall. 'I can't see, give me your binoculars,' she ordered Helen, who produced them from her rucksack with alacrity – but only for her own personal use. A small but fierce struggle ensued. 'She'll be *gone*,' Mum begged. 'Let me see.'

'Promise you'll give me a Valium and the gift of long vision is yours.'

It was a dilemma for Mum but she did the right thing.

'You know I can't do that,' she said primly and sat down on a couch. 'I'm your mother and it would be irresponsible.'

'Please yourself,' Helen said, then picked up the binoculars, gazed through them and murmured, 'Good Christ, would you look at that!' Then, 'Buh-loody *hell*! What are they trying to do? A tonsill*ectomy*?'

By then Mum had sprung off the couch and was trying to grab the binoculars from Helen and they both wrestled like children, only stopping when they bumped against my hand, the one with the missing fingernails and my shriek of pain restored them to decorum.

LISEY'S STORY
Stephen King
(For Nan Graham)

I

The spouses of well-known writers are almost invisible; no
one knows better than Lisey Landon, who has given only
one actual interview in her life. This was for the well-
known women's magazine that publishes the column 'Yes,
I'm Married to *Him!*' She spent roughly half of its five
hundred-word length explaining that her name (actually
short for Lisa) rhymes with 'CeeCee'. Most of the other
half had to do with her recipe for slow-cooked roast beef.
Her sister Amanda, who can be mean, said that the accompanying photograph made Lisey look fat.

There was another photograph, one that first appeared
in the Nashville *American* and then in newspapers
around the world, mostly under the headline HEROIC
GRADUATE STUDENT SAVES FAMOUS WRITER, or
variations thereof. This one shows a man in his early
twenties holding the handle of a shovel that looks almost
small enough to be a toy. The young fellow is peering at
it, and by his foozled expression the viewer might infer he

has no idea at all of what he's looking at. It could be an artillery shell, a bonsai tree, a radiation detector, or a china pig with a slot in its back for nickels. It could be a whang-dang-doodle, a cloche hat made out of coyote fur, or a phylactery testifying to the pompatus of love. A man in what looks like a *faux* Highway Patrolman's uniform (no gun, but you got your Sam Browne belt running across the chest and a good-sized badge, as well) is shaking the dazed young man's free hand. The cop – he *has* to be a cop of some kind, gun or not – has a huge oh-thank-God grin on his kisser, the kind that says *Son, you will never have to buy yourself another drink in a bar where I am, as long as we both shall live, so help me God, amen.* In the background, mostly out of focus, are staring people with dismayed what-the-hell-just-happened expressions of their faces.

And although thousands, perhaps even millions, of people have seen this photo, which has over the years become almost as famous as the one of the mortally wounded Lee Harvey Oswald clutching his belly, no one has ever noticed that the writer's wife is also in it.

Yes. Indeed she is. A part of her, anyway.

On the far right-hand side. Not quite halfway up.

If you look closely (a magnifying glass helps in this regard), you'll see half a shoe. Half a brown loafer. Half a *cordovan* loafer, to be exact, with a quarter-heel. Eighteen years later Lisey Landon can still remember how comfortable those shoes were, and how fast she moved in them that day. Faster than the award-winning photographer, certainly, and she'd not seen the dazed campus cop or the dazed young man – Tony, his name had been – at all. Not then, she hadn't. But she had earlier, and certainly later, in this picture, and how it had made her laugh. How it makes her laugh still. Because the spouses of well-known writers are almost always invisible.

But I got a shoe in there, she sometimes thinks. *I poked in a loafer. I did that much. Didn't I, Scott?*

Her position was always behind him at those ceremonial things; behind him and slightly to the right, with her hands demurely clasped before her. She remembers that very well.

She remembers it all very well, probably better than the rest of them. Probably better than any of them.

II

Lisey stands behind and slightly to Scott's right with her hands clasped demurely before her, watching her husband balance on one foot, the other on the silly little shovel which is half-buried in loose dirt that has clearly been brought in for the occasion. The day is hot, maddeningly humid, almost sickeningly muggy, and the considerable crowd that has gathered only makes matters worse. Unlike the dignitaries in attendance for the groundbreaking, the lookie-loo-come-'n'-see folk are not dressed in anything approaching their best, and while their jeans and shorts and pedal pushers may not exactly make them comfortable in the wet-blanket air, Lisey envies them just the same as she stands here at the crowd's forefront in the suck-oven heat of the Tennessee afternoon. Just standing pat, dolled up in her hot-weather best, is stressful: worrying that she'll soon be sweating big dark circles in the light brown linen top she's wearing over the blue rayon shell blouse. She's got on a great bra for hot weather and still it's biting into the undersides of her boobs. Happy days, babyluv.

Scott, meanwhile, continues balancing on one foot while

his hair, too long in back – he needs it cut badly, she knows that he looks in the mirror and sees a rock star but she looks at him and sees a dolled-up hobo out of a Woody Guthrie song – blows in the occasional hot puff of breeze. He's being a good sport while the photographer circles. *Damn* good sport. He's flanked on the left by a fellow named Tony Eddington, who is going to write up all this happy crappy for the something-or-other (campus newspaper? surely the campus newspaper goes on hiatus at least during the month of August, if not for the entire summer?), and on the right by their stand-in host, an English department stalwart named Roger Dashmiel, one of those men who seem older than they are not only because they have lost so much hair and gained so much belly so soon but because they insist upon drawing an almost stifling gravitas around themselves. Even their witticisms felt like oral readings of insurance policy clauses to Lisey.

Making matters worse in this case is the fact that Roger Dashmiel does not like her husband. Lisey has sensed this at once (it's easy, because most men do like him), and it's given her something upon which to focus her unease. For she *is* uneasy – profoundly so. She has tried to tell herself that it is no more than the humidity and the gathering clouds in the west presaging strong afternoon thunderstorms or maybe even tornadoes: a low-barometer thing, only that and nothing more. But the barometer wasn't low in Maine when she got out of bed this morning at quarter to seven; it had been a beautiful summer morning already, with the newly risen sun sparkling on a trillion points of dew in the field between the house and the barn which housed Scott's study. What her father, old Dandy Debusher, would have called 'a real ham 'n' egger of a day.' Yet the instant her feet touched the oak on her side of the bed and

her thoughts turned to the trip to Nashville – leave for the
Portland Jetport at eight, fly out on Delta at nine-thirty –
her heart dipped with dread and her morning-empty stomach, usually sweet, foamed with unmotivated fear. She'd
greeted these sensations with surprised dismay, because she
ordinarily *liked* to travel, especially with Scott: the two of
them sitting companionably side by side, he with his book
open, she with hers. Sometimes he'd read her a bit of his
and sometimes she'd vice him a little versa. Sometimes she'd
feel him and look up and find his eyes – his solemn regard.
As though she were a mystery to him still. Yes, and sometimes there would be turbulence, and she liked that, too. It
was like the rides at the Topsham Fair when she and her sisters had been young. Scott never minded the turbulence,
either. She remembered one particularly crazy approach
into Denver – strong winds, thunderheads, little prop-job
commuter-plane all over the sky – and how she'd looked
over to see him actually pogo-ing up and down in his seat
like a little kid who needs to go to the bathroom, with this
crazy grin on his face. No, the rides that scared Scott were
the smooth downbound ones he took in the middle of his
wakeful nights. Sometimes he talked (lucidly – smiling,
even) about things you could only see if you looked through
the fingerprints on a water glass. It scared her to hear him
talk like that. Because it was crazy, and because she sort of
knew what he meant and didn't want to.

So it wasn't low barometer that had been bothering her –
not then – and it certainly hadn't been the prospect of getting on one more airplane or eating one more airline snack
(these days she brought their own, anyway, usually homemade trail-mix). And then, in the bathroom, reaching for
the light over the sink – something she had done without
incident or accident day in and out for the entire eight

years they'd lived here, which came to approximately three thousand days, less time spent on the road – she smacked the toothglass with the back of her hand and sent it tumbling to the floor, where it shattered into approximately one million stupid pieces.

'Shit *fire*, save your smuckin' matches!' she cried, lips drawn back from her teeth, frightened and irritated to find herself so: for she did not believe in omens, not she, not Lisey Landon the writer's wife; not little Lisey Debusher, either. Omens were for the shanty Irish.

Scott, who had just come back into the bedroom with two cups of coffee and a plate of buttered toast on a tray, stopped dead. 'Whadja break, babyluv?'

'Nothing that came out of the dog's ass,' Lisey said savagely, and was then sort of astounded with herself. That was one of Granny Debusher's sayings, and Granny D certainly *had* believed in omens, but that old Irish highpockets had gone on the cooling board when Lisey was only four. Was it even possible Lisey could remember her? It seemed so, for as she stood there, looking down at the stupid shards of toothglass, the actual *articulation* of the omen came to her, came in Granny D's tobacco-strapped voice . . . and comes back now, as she stands watching her husband be a good sport in his lightest-weight summer sport coat (which he will soon be sweating through under the arms nevertheless): *broken glass in the morning, broken hearts at night.* That was Granny D's scripture, all right, handed down and remembered by at least one little girl before Granny D pitched down dead in the chicken yard with an apronful of feed and a sack of Bull Durham tied up inside her sleeve.

It isn't the heat, it isn't the trip, and it isn't Dashmiel, who only ended up doing the meet 'n' greet job because the head of the English department, with whom Scott had corresponded, is in the hospital following an emergency gall bladder removal the day before. It is a broken . . . smucking . . . *toothglass* at ten minutes to seven in the morning combined with the saying of a long-dead Irish granny. And the joke of it is, Scott will later point out, it's just enough to put her on edge, just enough to get her either strapped or at least semi-strapped.

Sometimes, he will tell her not long hence, speaking from a hospital bed (ah, but he could so easily have been on the cooling board himself, all his wakeful, too-thoughtful nights over) in his new high whistling and effortful voice, *sometimes just enough is just enough. As the saying is.*

And she knew exactly what he meant.

III

Roger Dashmiel has his share of headaches today, Lisey knows that. It doesn't make her like him any better, but sure, she knows. If there was ever an actual script for the ceremony, Professor Hegstrom (he of the emergency gall bladder attack) has been too muddled to tell Dashmiel what or where it is. Dashmiel has consequently been left with little more than a time of day and a cast of characters featuring a writer to whom he has taken an instant dislike. When the little party of dignitaries left Inman Hall, temporary home of the library sciences staff, for the short but exceedingly warm walk to the site of the forthcoming Shipman Library, Dashmiel told Scott they'd have to more or less play it by ear. Scott shrugged good-naturedly and nodded. He was absolutely comfortable with that. For Scott Landon, ear was a way of life.

'Ah'll introduce you,' Dashmiel said as they walked toward the baked and shimmering plot of land where the new library would stand. The photographer in charge of immortalizing all of this danced restlessly back and forth, hither and yon, snapping and snapping, busy as a gnat. Lisey could see a rectangle of fresh brown earth not far ahead, about nine feet by five, she judged, and pickup-trucked in that morning by the just-starting-to-fade look of it. No one had thought to put up an awning, and already the surface of the fresh dirt had acquired a grayish glaze.

'*Somebody* better do it,' Scott said.

Dashmiel had frowned as if wounded by some unde-served canard. Then, with a sigh, he pressed on. 'Applause follows introduction – '

'As day follows night,' Scott murmured.

'– and then yew'll say a woid or tew,' Dashmiel finished. Beyond the baked tract of land awaiting the library, a fresh-ly paved parking-lot shimmered in the sunlight, all smooth tar and staring yellow lines. Lisey saw fantastic ripples of nonexistent water on its far side.

'My pleasure,' Scott said.

The unvarying good nature of his responses seemed to worry Dashmiel rather than reassure him. 'Ah hope yew won't want to say *tew* much at the groundbreakin',' he told Scott rather severely as they approached the roped-off area. This had been kept clear, but there was a crowd big enough to stretch almost to the parking lot waiting beyond it. An even larger one had trailed Dashmiel and the Landons from Inman Hall. Soon the two would merge, and Lisey – who ordinarily did not mind crowds any more than she minded turbulence at twenty thousand feet – didn't like this, either. It occurred to her that so many people on a day this hot might suck all the air out of the air. Totally dopey idea, but –

'It's mahty hot, even for Naishveel in August, wouldn't you say so, Toneh?'

Tony Eddington – who would be *rahtin all this up* for something called the U-Tenn *Review* – nodded obligingly but said nothing. His only comment so far had been to identify the tirelessly dancing photographer as Stefan Queensland, U-Tenn Nashville, class of '83, currently of the Nashville *American*. 'Hope y'all will h'ep him out if y'can,' Tony Eddington had said softly to Scott as they began their walk over here. Eddington was carrying a little wire notebook in which he had so far written absolutely nothing, so far as Lisey could see.

'Yew'll finish yoah remarks,' Dashmiel said, 'and there'll be anothuh round of applause. Then, Mistuh Landon – '

'Scott.'

Dashmiel had flashed a rictus grin, there for just a moment, then gone. 'Then, *Scott*, yew'll go on and toin that all-impawtant foist shovelful of oith.' *Toin? Foist? Oith?* Lisey mused, and then it came to her that Dashmiel was saying *turn that all-important first shovelful of earth* in his only semi-believable Louisiana drawl. 'Followin' that, we'll proceed on across yonduh parkin' lot to Nelson Hall – which is mercifully air-conditioned, Ah might add.'

'All sounds fine to me,' Scott replied, and that was all he had time for, because they had arrived.

IV

Perhaps it's a holdover from the broken toothglass – that *omenish* feeling – but the plot of trucked-in dirt looks like a grave to Lisey: XL size, as if for a giant. The two crowds collapse in around it in a circle, becoming one and creating that breathless suck-oven feel at the center. A campus security guard now stands at each corner of the ornamental velvet-rope barrier, beneath which Dashmiel, Scott, and 'Toneh' Eddington have ducked. Queensland, the photographer, dances relentlessly, his old-fashioned Speed Graphic held up in front of his face. There are big patches of darkness under his arms and a sweat-tree growing up the back of his shirt. *Paging Weegee*, Lisey thinks, and realizes she envies him. He is so free, flitting gnatlike in the heat; he is twenty-five and all his shit still works. Dashmiel, however, is looking at him with growing impatience which Stefan Queensland affects not to see until he has exactly the shot he wants. Lisey has an idea it's one of Scott alone, his foot on the silly silver spade, his hair blowing back in the breeze. In any case, Weegee Junior at last lowers his big old box of a camera and steps back to the edge of the crowd's far curve. And here, following him with her somewhat wistful regard, Lisey first sees the madman, a graduate student with long blonde hair named Gerd Allen Cole. He has the look, one local reporter will later write, 'of John Lennon recovering from his romance with heroin – hollow eyes at odd and disquieting contrast to his puffy child's cheeks.'

At that moment, beyond noting all that tumbled blonde hair, Lisey thinks nothing of Gerd Allen Cole, *omens* or no *omens*. She just wants this to be over so she can find a bathroom stall in the bowels of the English department across the way and pull her rebellious underwear out of the crack of her ass. She has to make water, too, but right now that's pretty much secondary.

'*Ladies and gentlemen!*' Dashmiel says in the carrying

but somehow artificial voice of a carnival barker, *'It is mah distinct pleasure to introduce Mr Scott Landon, authuh of the Pulitzuh Prize-winnin'* Relics *and the National Book Award winnin'* The Coster's Daughter. *He's come all the way from Maine with his loveleh wife to inauguarate construction – yes, at long last – on our vereh own Shipman Lah-brey! Scott Landon, folks! Let's hear it!'*

The crowd applauds at once, and enthusiastically. The loveleh wife joins in, patting her palms together automatically, looking at Dashmiel and thinking, *He won the NBA for* The Coster's Daughter. *That's* Coster, *not* Coster. *And I sort of think you knew it. Why don't you like him, you petty man?*

Then she happens to glance beyond him and this time she really *does* notice Gerd Allen Cole. He is just standing there with all that fabulous blonde hair tumbled down to his eyebrows and the sleeves of a white shirt far too big for him – he's all but floating in it – rolled up to his biceps. The tails of this shirt are out and dangle almost to the whitened knees of the old jeans he wears. Instead of applauding Blondie has got his hands clasped rather prissily together in front of him and there's a spooky-sweet smile on his face and his lips are moving, as if he's saying a prayer . . . but he's looking straight at Scott. As the wife of a public man (some of the time, at least), Lisey at once pegs Blondie as a potential problem. She thinks of guys like this as 'deep-space fans', although she'd never say so out loud and has never even told Scott this. Deep-space fans always have a lot to say. They want to grab Scott by the arm and tell him that that they understand the secret messages in his books; deep-space fans know the books are really secret guides to God, Satan, or possibly the Coptic Gospels. They might be on about Scientology or numerology. Sometimes they want to talk about other worlds – secret worlds. Two years ago a deep-space fan hitchhiked all the way from Texas to Maine to talk to Scott about Bigfoot. That guy made Lisey a little nervous – there was a certain wall-eyed look of *absence* about him, and a knife (sheathed, thank Christ) in one of the loops of his backpack – but Scott talked to him a little, gave him a beer, took a couple of his pamphlets, signed the kid a paperback copy of *Instructions To Be Left In Earth*, clapped him on the back, and sent him on his way, happy. Sometimes – when he's got it strapped on nice and tight – Scott is amazing. No other word will do.

The thought of actual violence does not now occur to Lisey – certainly not the idea that Blondie means to pull a Mark David Chapman on her husband. *My mind just doesn't run that way*, she might have said.

Scott acknowledges the applause – and a few raucous rebel yells – with the Scott Landon grin which has been caricatured in the *Wall Street Journal* (it will later appear on any number of Barnes & Noble shopping bags), all the time continuing to balance on one foot while the other holds its place on the shoulder of the silly shovel. He lets the applause run for ten or fifteen seconds, whatever his intuition tells him is right (and his intuition is rarely wrong), then raises one hand, waving it off. And it goes. When he speaks, his voice seems nowhere near as loud as Dashmiel's, but Lisey knows that even with no mike or battery-powered bullhorn – and the lack of either here this afternoon is probably someone's oversight – it will carry to the very back rows of the crowd. And the crowd helps out. It's gone absolutely silent, straining to hear him: every golden word. A Famous Man has come among them. A Thinker and a Writer. He will now scatter pearls of wisdom before them.

Pearls before swine, Lisey thinks. *Sweaty swine, at that.* But didn't her father once tell her that pigs don't sweat? She can't exactly remember, and it's sort of an odd train of thought anyway, isn't it?

Across from her, Blondie carefully pushes his tumbled hair back from a fine white brow with his left hand. Then he clasps the left with his right again. His hands are as white as his brow and Lisey thinks: *there's one piggy who stays inside a lot. A stay-at-home swine, and why not? He looks like he's got all* sorts *of strange deep-space ideas to catch up on.*

She shifts from one foot to the other, and the silk of her underwear all but *squeaks* in the crack of her ass. Oh, maddening! She forgets Blondie again in trying to calculate if she might not . . . while Scott's making his remarks . . . very surreptitiously, mind you . . .

Her dead mother speaks up. Dour. Three words. Brooking no argument. *No, Lisey. Wait.*

'Ain't gonna sermonize, me,' Scott says, and she recognizes the patois of Gully Foyle, the main character in his all-time favorite novel, Alfred Bester's *The Demolished Man*. 'Too hot for sermons.'

'*Beam us up, Scotty!*' someone in the fifth or sixth row on the parking-lot side of the crowd yells exuberantly. The crowd laughs and cheers.

'Can't do it, brother,' Scott says, 'transporters are broken and we're all out of lithium crystals.'

The crowd, being new to the riposte as well as the sally (Lisey has heard both at least fifty times; maybe as many as a hundred), roars its approval and applauds. Across the way, Blondie smiles thinly, sweatlessly, and continues to grip his left hand with his right. And now Scott does take his foot off the spade, not as if he's grown impatient with it but as if he has, for the moment, found another use for the tool. She watches, not without fascination, for this is Scott at his best, not reading scripture but strutting show-time.

'It's nineteen-eighty-six and the world has grown dark,' he says. He slips the three feet or so of the little spade's wooden handle easily through his cupped hand, so that his fingers rest near the thing's business end. The scoop winks sun in Lisey's eyes once, and then it is mostly hidden by the sleeve of Scott's lightweight jacket. With the scoop and the blade hidden, he uses the slim wooden handle as a pointer, ticking off trouble and tragedy in the air in front of him.

'In January, the *Challenger* shuttle explodes, killing all seven on board. Bad call on a cold morning, folks. They never should have tried to launch.

'In February, at least thirty die on Election Day in the Phillipines. Ferdinand and Imelda Marcos, meanwhile, responsible for the deaths of a hundred times that number – maybe four hundred times that number – leave for Guam and, eventually, Hawaii. No one knows how many pairs of shoes babyluv takes with her.'

There's a ripple of laughter from the crowd. Not much. Tony Eddington is finally taking notes. Roger Dashmiel looks hot and put out with this unexpected current-events lesson.

'The nuclear reactor accident at Chernobyl kills thou-sands, sickens tens of thousands.

'The AIDS epidemic kills thousands, sickens tens of thousands.

'The world grows dark. Discordia rises. Mr Yeats's blood-tide is still undimmed.'

He looks down, looks fixedly at nil but graying earth, and Lisey is suddenly terrified that he is seeing it, his private monster, the thing with the endless patchy piebald side, that he is going to go off, perhaps even come to the break she knows he is afraid of (in truth she is as afraid of it as he is) in front of all these people. Then, before her heart can do more than begin to speed up, he raises his head, grins like a boy at the county fair, and shoots the handle of the spade through his fist to the halfway point. It's a showy move, a poolshark's move, and the folks at the front of the crowd go *ooooh*. But Scott's not done. Holding the spade out before him, he rotates the handle nimbly in his fingers, accelerating it into an unlikely spin. It's a baton-twirler's move, as dazzling – because of the silver scoop swinging in the sun, mostly – as it is unexpected. She's been married to him since 1977 – almost nine years now – and had no *idea* he had such a sublimely cool move in his repertoire. (How many years does it take, she'll wonder later, lying in bed alone in her substandard motel room and listening to dogs bark beneath a hot orange Nashville moon, before the simple stupid weight of time finally sucks all the wow out of a marriage?) The silver bowl of the rapidly swinging spade sends a *Wake up! Wake up!* sunflash running across the heat-dazed, sweat-sticky surface of the crowd. Lisey's husband is suddenly Scott the Pitchman, grinning, and she has never been so relieved to see that totally untrustworthy *honey, I'm hip* huckster's grin on her husband's face. He has bummed them out; now he will sell them the doubtful good cheer with which he hopes to send them home. And she thinks they will buy, hot August afternoon or not. When he's like this, Scott could sell Frigidaires to Inuits, as the saying is . . . and God bless the language pool where we all go first to drink our fill and then to strap on our business.

'But if every book is a little light in that darkness – and

151

so I believe, so I believe, so I must believe, for I write the goddam things, don't I? – then every library is a grand bonfire around which ten thousand people come to stand and warm themselves each cold day and night. We celebrate the laying of such a fire this afternoon, and I'm honored to be a part of it. Here is where we spit in the eye of chaos and kick murder right in his wrinkled old *cojones. Hey, photographer!'*

Stefan Queensland snaps to, but smiling.

Scott, also smiling, says: 'Now – get one of this. The powers that be may not want to use it, but you'll like it in your portfolio, I'll bet.'

Scott holds the ornamental tool out as if he intends to twirl it again, and the crowd gives a little hopeful gasp, but he's only teasing them. He slides his left hand back down to the spade's collar, his right to a position on the handle about a foot from the top. Then he bends, digs in, and drives the spade-blade deep, dousing its hot glitter in earth. He brings it up, tosses its dark load aside, and cries: '*I declare the Shipman Library construction site OPEN!'*

The applause that greets this makes the previous rounds sound like the sort of polite patter you might hear at a prep-school tennis match. Lisey doesn't know if young Mr Queensland caught the ceremonial first scoop, not for sure (she wasn't looking), but when Scott pumps the silly little silver spade at the sky like an Olympic hero, Queensland catches that one for sure, laughing as he snaps it. Scott holds the pose for a moment (Lisey happens to glance at Dashmiel and catches that gentleman in the act of rolling his eyes at Mr Eddington – Toneh). Then he lowers the spade to port arms and holds it that way, grinning. Sweat has popped on his cheeks and brows in fine beads. The applause begins to taper off. The crowd thinks he's done.

Lisey, who can read him like a book (as the saying is), knows better.

When they can hear him again, Scott bends down for an encore scoop. 'This one's for Yeats!' he calls. Another scoop. 'This one's for Poe!' Yet another scoop. 'This one's for Alfred Bester, and if you haven't read him, you ought to be ashamed!' He's starting to sound out of breath, and Lisey, although mostly still amused, is starting to feel a bit alarmed, as well. It's *so* hot. She's trying to remember what he ate for lunch – was it heavy or light?

'And this one . . . ' He dives the spade into what is now a fairly respectable little divot (Queensland documenting each fresh foray) one last time and holds up the final dip of earth. The front of his shirt has darkened with sweat. 'Well, why don't you think of whoever wrote your favorite book? The one that, in a perfect world, you'd check out first when the Shipman Library finally opens its doors to you? Got it? Okay – this one's for him, or her, or them.' He tosses the dirt aside, gives the spade a final valedictory shake, then turns to Dashmiel . . . who should be pleased with Scott's showmanship, Lisey thinks – asked to play by ear, Scott has played brilliantly – and who instead only looks hot and pissed off. 'I think we're done here,' he says, and makes as if to hand Dashmiel the spade.

'No, that's yoahs,' Dashmiel says. 'As a keepsake, and a token of ouah thanks. Along with yoah check, of co'se.' His smile – the rictus, not the real one – comes and goes in a fitful cramp. 'Shall we go and grab ow'sefs a little air-con-ditionin?'

'By all means,' Scott says, looking bemused, and then hands the spade to Lisey – as he has handed her so many other mostly unwanted mementos over the past twelve years of his celebrity: everything from ceremonial oars and

Boston Red Sox hats encased in Lucite cubes to the masks of comedy and tragedy . . . but mainly pen-and-pencil sets. So many pen-and-pencil sets. Waterman, Scripto, Schaeffer, Montblanc, you name it. She looks at the spade's glittering silver scoop, as bemused as her beloved (he is still her beloved, and she's come to believe he always will be). Every last speck of dirt has slid off, it seems; even the blade is clean. There are a few flecks in the incised letters reading COMMENCEMENT, SHIPMAN LIBRARY, and Lisey blows them off. Then she looks at this unlikely prize again. Where will such an artifact end up? She'd say Scott's study over the barn, but in this summer of 1986 the study is still under construction and probably won't be ready for occupancy until October . . . although the address works and he has already begun to store stuff in the musty stalls of the barn below. Across many of the cardboard boxes he had scrawled SCOTT! THE EARLY YEARS! Most likely the silver spade will wind up with this stuff, wasting its gleams in the gloom. The one depressing surety is that it'll wind up in a place where one of them will stumble across it twenty years from now and try to remember just *what* in the blue *smuck* –

Meanwhile, Dashmiel is on the move. Without another word – as if he's disgusted with this whole business and determined to put it behind him as soon as possible – he starts across the rectangle of fresh earth, detouring around the divot which Scott's last big shovelful of earth has almost succeeded in promoting to a hole. The heels of Dashmiel's shiny black I'm-an-assistant-professor-on-my-way-up-and-you're-not shoes sink deep into the earth with every step. Dashmiel has to fight for balance, and Lisey guesses this does nothing to improve his mood. Tony Eddington falls in beside him. Scott pauses a moment, as if not quite sure what's going on, and then also starts to move, slipping himself in between Dashmiel and Eddington. He delighted her into forgetting her *omenish* feeling

(*broken glass in the morning*)

for a little while, but now it's back

(*broken hearts at night*)

and with a vengeance. She thinks it must be why all these details look so *big* to her. She is sure the world will come back into more normal focus once she has, in Dashmiel's words, grabbed herself a little air-conditioning. And once she's gotten that pesty swatch of cloth out of her butt.

This really is almost over, she reminds herself, and – how funny life can be – it is at this precise moment that the day begins to derail.

A campus security cop who is older than the others on this detail (she will later identify him from Stefan Queensland's news photo as Captain S. Heffernan) holds up the rope barrier on the far side of the ceremonial rectangle of earth. All she notices about him is that he's wearing what her husband might have called *a puffickly huh-yooge batch of orifice* on his khaki shirt. Her husband and his two flanking escorts – Dashmiel on Scott's left, C. Anthony Eddington on Scott's right – duck beneath the rope in a move so synchronized it almost could have been choreographed.

The crowd is moving toward the parking lot with the principals . . . with one exception. *Blondie* is not heading toward the parking lot. Blondie is still standing on the parking-lot side of the commencement patch. A few people bump him, and he's forced a few steps backward after all, on to the baked dead earth where the Shipman Library will stand come 1989 (if the chief contractor's promises can be believed, that is). Then he's actually stepping forward against the tide, his hands coming unclasped so he can push first a girl out of his way to his left and then a guy out of his way on his right. His mouth is moving. At first Lisey again thinks he's mouthing a silent prayer, and then she hears the broken gibberish – like something a bad James Joyce imitator might write – and for the first time she becomes actively alarmed. Blondie's somehow weird blue eyes are fixed on her husband, but Lisey understands that he does not want to discuss Bigfoot or the hidden religious subtexts of Scott's novels. This is no mere deep-space boy.

'The churchbells came down Angel Street thick as falling oak trees,' says Blondie – says Gerd Allen Cole – who, it will turn out, spent most of his seventeenth year in an expensive Virginia mental institution and was released as cured and good to go, thanks very much, and these words Lisey gets in the clear. They cut through the rising chatter of the crowd, that hum of conversation, like a knife through some light, sweet cake. 'That rungut sound, ar! Like rain on a tin roof! Dirty flowers! Ya, dirty and sweet! This is how the church bells sound in the basement!'

A right hand that seems made entirely of long pale fingers goes to the tails of the white shirt, and Lisey suddenly understands

(*George Wallace oh Christ Wallace and Bremmer*)

exactly what's going on here, although it comes to her in a series of shorthand TV images from her childhood. She looks at Scott and sees Scott is speaking to Dashmiel. Dashmiel is looking at Stefan Queensland, the irritated frown on Dashmiel's face saying he's had *Quite! Enough! Photographs! For One Day! Thank! You!* Queensland himself is looking down at his camera, making some adjustment, and C. Anthony 'Toneh' Eddington is making a note on his pad. She even spies the older campus security cop, he of the khaki uniform and the puffickly *huh-yooge* batch of orifice; this worthy is looking at the crowd, but it is *the wrong part* of the crowd. It's impossible that she can see all these folks and Blondie too, but she can, she does; she can even see Scott's lips forming the words *think that went pretty well*, which is a testing comment he often makes after events like this . . . and oh Jesus Mary and JoJo the Carpenter, she tries to scream out Scott's name and warn him but *her throat locks up*, dry and spitless, she can't say anything, and Blondie's got the tails of that lolloping big white shirt all the way up, and underneath are empty belt loops and a flat hairless belly and lying against his white skin is the butt of a gun which he now lays hold of and she hears him say, closing in on Scott a little from the right, 'If it closes the lips of the bells, it will have done the job. I'm sorry Papa.'

I'm sorry Papa.

She's running forward, or trying to, but oh God she's got such a puffickly *huh-yooge* case of gluefoot and someone shoulders in front of her, a coed with her hair tied up in a wide white silk ribbon with NASHVILLE printed on it in blue (see how she sees everything?), and Lisey pushes her with one hand, the hand not holding the silver spade, and the coed caws '*Hey!*', except it sounds slower and draggier than that, like the word *hey* recorded at 45 RPM and then played back at 33 1/3 or maybe even 16 RPM. The whole world has gone to hot tar and for an eternity Scott and Dashmiel are blocked from her view; she can only see Tony Eddington, making more of his idiotic notes – a slow starter, but once he gets going . . . whooo! Boy takes notes like a house afire! Then the coed with the NASHVILLE ribbon stumbles clear of Lisey's field of vision – *finally!* –

and as Dashmiel and her husband come into view again, Lisey sees Dashmiel's body language go from a drone to a startled cry of fear. It happens in the space of an instant.

Lisey sees what Dashmiel sees. She sees Blondie now with the gun (it will prove to be a Ladysmith .22, made in Korea and bought at a pawn-and-loan in South Nashville for thirty-seven dollars) pointed at her husband, who has at last seen his danger and stopped. In Lisey-time, all of this happens very, very slowly. She doesn't actually see the bullet fly out of the .22's muzzle – not quite – but she hears Scott say, very mildly, seeming to drawl the words over the course of ten or even fifteen seconds: 'Let's talk about it, son, right?' And then she sees fire bloom from the gun's nickel-plated muzzle in a yellow-white corsage. She hears a pop – a stupid, insignificant: the sound of someone breaking a paper lunch sack with the palm of his hand. She sees Dashmiel, that chickenshit southern-fried asshole, turn and plunge away to his immediate left. She sees Scott buck backward on his heels. At the same time his chin thrusts forward. The combination is weirdly graceful, like a dance-floor move. A black hole opens in the right side of his summer sport coat. 'Son, you honest-to-God don't want to do that,' he says, and even in Lisey-time she hears the way his voice thins a little more on every word until he sounds like a test pilot in a high-altitude chamber. Yet Lisey is almost positive he doesn't know he has been shot. His sport coat swings open as he puts his hand out in a commanding *stop-this-shit* gesture, and she realizes two things simultaneously: that she can see gouts of blood soaking into the front of his shirt and that she has at last – oh thank God for small favors – broken into some semblance of a run.

'I got to end all this ding-dong for the freesias,' says Gerd Allen Cole with perfect fretful clarity, and Lisey is suddenly sure that once Scott is dead, once the damage is done, Blondie will either kill himself or pretend to try. For the time being, however, he has this first business to finish. The business of the author. Blondie turns his wrist slightly so that the smoking and somehow cuntish muzzle of the Ladysmith .22 points at the left side of Scott's chest; in Lisey-time the move is smooth and slow. Blondie has done the lung; his second bullet will be a heart-shot, she thinks, and knows she can't allow that to happen. If her husband is to have any chance at all, this loony tune must not be allowed to put any more lead into him.

As if hearing her, repudiating her, Gerd Allen Cole says, 'It never ends until you are. You're responsible for all these repetitions, old boy. You are hell, and you are a monkey, and now you are *my* monkey!'

This speech is the closest he comes to making sense, and making it gives Lisey just enough time to first wind up with the silver spade – her hands, somehow knowing their business in their own way, have already found their position near the top of the thing's forty-inch handle – and then swing it. Still, it's close. If it had been a horse race, the tote board would undoubtedly have flashed the HOLD TICK-ETS WAIT FOR PHOTO message. But when the race is between a man with a gun and a woman with a shovel, you don't need a photo. And in slowed-down Lisey-time there's no chance of a missed perception, anyway. She sees it all. She sees the spade's silver scoop strike the gun, driving it upward, just as that corsage blooms again (she can see only part of the flame and none of the muzzle; the muzzle is hidden by the blade of the spade). She sees the spade carry on forward and upward as the second shot goes harmless-ly into the hot August sky. She sees the gun fly loose, and there is time to think *Holy smuck! I really put a charge into this one!* before the commemorative spade connects with the blonde fruitcake's face. His hand is still in there (three of those slim long fingers will be broken and Lisey could give Shit One about Monsieur Deep-Space Fruitcake Cole's fingers), but all the hand ends up protecting is his forehead. The spade's silver bowl connects solidly with the lower part of the would-be assassin's face, breaking his nose, shattering his right cheekbone and the bony orbit around his staring right eye, mashing his lips back against his teeth (and pretty well exploding the upper lip), breaking nine teeth, as well – the four in front will prove to be shattered right down to the gumline. All in all, it's quite a job. A Mafia goon with a set of brass knucks couldn't have done better.

Now – still slow, still in Lisey-time – the elements of Stefan Queensland's award-winning photograph are assembling themselves.

Captain S. Heffernan has seen what's happening only a second or two after Lisey, but he has also had to deal with the bystander problem, in his case a fat bepimpled fella wearing baggy Bermuda shorts and a T-shirt with Scott Landon's smiling face on the front. Captain Heffernan first grapples with this young fella and then shunts him aside with one muscular shoulder. The young fella goes flying with a dismayed *what-the-fuck?* expression on the speckled moon face beneath his crew cut.

By then Lisey has administered the silver spade to the would-be assassin. Gerd Allen Cole, aka Blondie, is sinking to the ground (and out of the photo's field) with a dazed expression in one eye and blood pouring from the other one. Blood is also gushing from the hole that was his mouth. Heffernan completely misses the actual hit.

Roger Dashmiel, suddenly remembering that he is supposed to be the master of ceremonies and not a jackrabbit, turns back toward Eddington, his protégé, and Landon, his troublesome guest of honor, just in time to take his place as a staring, slightly blurred face in the photo's background.

Scott Landon, meanwhile, shock-walks right out of the award-winning photo. He walks as though unmindful of the heat, striding toward the parking lot and Nelson Hall beyond, Nelson Hall which is home of the English department, and air-conditioned. He walks with surprising briskness, at least to begin with, and a goodly part of the crowd moves with him. The crowd seems for the most part unaware that anything has happened. Lisey is both infuriated and unsurprised. After all, how many of them actually saw Blondie with that cuntish little pistol in his hand? How many of them recognized the burst-paper-bag sounds as gunshots? The hole in Scott's coat could be a smudge of dirt from his shoveling chore, and the blood which has soaked his shirt is as yet invisible to the outside world. He's now making a strange and horrible whistling noise each time he inhales, but how many of them hear that? No, it's *her* they're looking at – some of them, anyway – the daffy dame who has just inexplicably hauled off and smacked some guy in the face with the ceremonial silver spade. A lot of them are grinning about it, actually *grinning*, as if they believe it's all part of a show being put on for their benefit; the Scott Landon Road Show. Probably they believe *exactly* that. Well, fuck them, and fuck Dashmiel, and fuck the day-late and dollar-short campus cop with his Sam Browne belt and oversize badge. All she cares about now is Scott. She thrusts the shovel out not quite blindly to her right and Eddington, their Boswell-for-a-day, takes it. It's either that or get smacked in the nose with it. Then, still in that dreadful slow-time, Lisey runs after her husband, whose briskness evaporates as soon as he reaches the suck-oven heat of the parking lot. He begins to stagger and weave; his upper body begins to curl into a shrimp-shape. She sees this and tries to run faster and still it feels like she's running in glue. Behind her, Tony Eddington is peering at the silver spade like a man who has no idea what he's gotten hold of; it might be an artillery shell, a radiation detector, or the Great Lost Whang-Dang-Doodle of the Egyptian Pharaohs. To him comes Captain S. Heffernan, and although Captain Heffernan will later in his secret heart *doubt* that it was really Eddington who laid the gun-toting nutjob low, the captain is not (even at one in the morning, even to himself, over bourbon and branch water), able to *swear* it was not Eddington but the wife who stopped the nutjob's clock before said nutjob could fire a second shot – the kill shot, most likely – into the writer. The mind is a monkey; the mind is a monster. The mind is sort of a madman, actually. Captain S. Heffernan knows these things, knows it's why so-called 'eyeball witnesses' are never to be trusted, and that includes so-called professionals like himself. *Besides*, he tells himself, *that fat kid with the zitzes and the crewcut was in my way.*

In any case, the nutjob is down, the nutjob is puling through the hole that used to be his mouth, the nutjob is toast, and Stan Heffernan seizes the Eddington kid's free left hand and pumps it, feeling a large relieved grin spread across his face as he realizes he may just get out of this mess with his skin on and his job intact.

Lisey runs toward her husband, who has just gone down on his hands and knees in the parking lot. And Queensland snaps his picture as she goes, catching just half of one shoe

on the far righthand side of the frame . . . something not
even he will realize, then or ever.

V

He goes down, the Pulitzer Prize winner goes down, Scott
Landon goes down, and Lisey makes the supreme effort to
break out of that slow and terrible Lisey-time. She must
succeed because she has heard the cry of alarm from the
part of the crowd that's been moving with Scott and now
she hears – in the maddening slow-speak of Lisey-time –
someone saying *Heeeeee's hurrrrt!* She must break free
because if she doesn't get to him before the crowd sur-
rounds him and shuts her out, they will very likely kill him
with their concern. With smotherlove.

She screams at herself in her own head

(*strap it on RIGHT NOW!*)

and that does it. Suddenly she is *knifing* forward; all the
world is noise and heat and sweat, but she blesses the
speedy reality of it even as she uses her left hand to grab the
left cheek of her ass and *pull*, raking the goddamn underwear out of the crack of her ass, there, at least one thing
about this wrong and broken day is now mended.

A coed in a shell top, the kind of top where the straps tie
on the shoulders in big floppy bows, threatens to block her
narrowing path to Scott, but Lisey ducks beneath her and
hits the hot-top. She will not be aware of her scraped and
blistered knees until much later – until the hospital, in fact,
where a kindly paramedic will notice and put lotion on
them, something so cool and soothing it will make her cry
with relief. But that is for later. Now it might as well be just
her and Scott alone here on the edge of this hot parking
lot, this terrible black-and-yellow ballroom floor which

must be a hundred and thirty degrees at least, maybe a hundred and fifty. Maybe more. Her mind tries to present her with the image of an egg frying sunny-side up in her Ma's old black iron spider and she thrusts it away. Scott looks up at her and now his face is waxy pale except for the black triangles forming beneath his eyes and the blood which has begun running from the right side of his mouth and down his chin in a scarlet stream.

'Lisey!' His voice is thin, whooping. 'Did he . . . shoot me?'

'Don't try to talk,' she tells him, and puts a hand on his chest. His shirt, oh dear God, it is not wet with blood but *soaked* with blood, and beneath it she can feel his heart running along so fast and light; it is not the heartbeat of a human being, she thinks, but that of a bird. *Pigeon-pulse*, she thinks, and that is when the girl with the floppy bows tied on her shoulders falls on top of her. She would land on Scott but Lisey instinctively shields him, taking the brunt of the girl's weight ('*Hey, shit! FUCK!*' the startled girl cries out) with her back . . . it is there for a moment and then gone. Lisey sees the girl shoot her hands out to break her fall – *oh, the divine reflexes of the young,* she thinks – and the girl is successful . . . but then she is crying, '*Ow! Ow! OW!*' This makes Lisey look at her own hands. They aren't blistered, not yet, but they *have* gone the deep red of a perfectly cooked Maine lobster.

'Lisey,' Scott whispers, and oh Christ how his breath *screams* when he pulls it in.

'*Who pushed me?*' the girl with the bows on her shoulders is demanding. She is a-hunker, hair from a busted ponytail in her eyes, crying with surprise, pain, and embarrassment.

Lisey leans close to Scott. The heat of him terrifies her

and fills her with pity deeper than any she has ever felt, deeper than she thought it was possible to feel. He is actually *shivering* with the heat. Awkwardly, using only one arm, she strips off her jacket. 'Scott, don't try to talk. You're right, you've been sh – '

'I'm so hot,' he says, and begins to shiver harder. What comes next – convulsions? His hazel eyes stare up into her blue ones. Blood runs from the corner of his mouth. She can smell it. It stinks. Now the collar of his shirt is filling in red. 'I'm so hot, please give me ice.'

'I will,' she says, and puts her jacket under his head and neck. 'I will, Scott.' *Thank God for his sport coat,* she thinks, not quite incoherent, and then has an idea. She grabs the hunkering, crying girl by the arm. 'What's your name?'

The girl stares at her as if she were mad, but answers the question. 'Lisa Lemke.'

Same as mine, small world, Lisey thinks, but does not say. What she says is, 'My husband has been shot, Lisa. Can you go over there to' – she cannot remember the name of the building, only its function – 'to the English department and call an ambulance? Dial 911 – '

'Ma'am? Mrs Landon, is it?' This is the campus security cop, making his way through the crowd with a lot of help from his meaty elbows. He squats beside her and his knees pop loudly. *His knees are louder than Blondie's pistol,* Lisey marvels. He's holding his walkie-talkie, which was previously clipped to his Sam Browne belt in the place where a regular cop would wear his gun. When he speaks, he does so slowly and carefully, as though to a distressed child. 'Mrs Landon, I have called the campus infirmary. They are rolling their ambulance, which will take your husband to Nashville Memorial. Nashville . . . Memorial . . . Hospital. Do you understand me?'

She does, and her gratitude to this man is almost as deep as the pity she feels for her husband, lying on the simmering pavement and bleeding from his chest and mouth, shuddering in the heat like a distempered dog. She nods, weeping the first of what will be many tears before she gets Scott back to Maine – not on a Delta flight but on a private jet, and with a private nurse, and with another ambulance and another private nurse to meet them at the Portland Jetport's Civil Aviation Terminal. And all that is later. Now she turns back to the Lemke girl and says, 'Lisey, he's burning up – is there ice, honey? Can you think of anywhere there might be ice?'

She says this without much hope, and is therefore amazed when Lisa Lemke nods at once. 'There's a soda machine and two snack machines over there.' She points in the direction of Nelson Hall, which Lisey can't see. All she can see is a crowding forest of bare legs, some hairy, some smooth, some tanned, some sunburned. She realizes they are completely hemmed in, that she's tending her fallen husband in a slot the shape of a large vitamin pill or cold capsule, and feels a touch of crowd-panic. Is the word for that agoraphobia? Scott would know.

'If you can get him some ice, please do,' Lisey says. 'And hurry.' She looks at the campus security cop, who has gone to one knee on Scott's other side and appears to be taking his pulse – a completely useless activity, in Lisey's opinion. 'Can't you make them move back?' she almost pleads. 'It's so *hot* – '

He doesn't give her time to finish, but is up like Jack from his box, yelling 'Move it back! Let this girl through! Move it back! Let this girl through! Let him breathe, folks, let him breathe, all right, what do you say?'

The crowd shuffles back . . . very reluctantly, Lisey

thinks. They want to see all the blood, it seems to her.

The heat bakes relentlessly up from the pavement. She has half-expected to get used to it, the way you get used to a hot shower, but that isn't happening. She listens for the approaching howl of the promised ambulance and hears nothing. Then she hears Scott, croaking her name. At the same time he twitches weakly at the side of the sweat-soaked shell top she's wearing (her bra now stands out against the silk as stark as a swollen tattoo). She looks down at him and sees something she does not like: Scott is smiling. The blood has coated his lips a rich candy red, top to bottom, side to side, and consequently the smile looks like the grin of a clown. *No one loves a clown at midnight*, she thinks, and wonders where *that* came from. It will only be much later that night – that long and mostly sleepless night, listening to the August dogs howl at the hot moon – that she'll realize it was Lon Chaney. She knows because the line was the epigram of Scott's third novel, the only one she has hated, *Empty Devils*. The one that's sort of a riff on Romero's *Living Dead* movies.

'Lisey.'

'Scott, don't try to talk – '

But he is relentless, twitching at her blue silk top, his eyes – dear God, they are so deep in their sockets now, but still so brilliant and fevery. He has something to say. And as always when he has something to say, he will find an audience if he can. This time he has her.

Reluctantly, she leans down.

For a moment he says nothing, but she can hear him getting ready to. He pulls air in a little at a time, in half gasps. The smell of blood is even stronger up close. A mineral smell. Or maybe it's detergent. Or –

It's death, Lisey, that's all. Just the smell of death.

As if he needs to ratify this, Scott says: 'It's very close, honey. I can't see it, but I . . .' Another long, screaming intake of breath. 'I hear it taking its meal. And grunting.' Smiling as he says it.

'Scott, I don't know what you're tal – '

The hand which has been tugging at her top now pinches her side, and cruelly – when she takes the top off much later, in the motel room, she'll see the bruise: a true lover's knot.

'You . . . ' Screamy breath. '*Know* . . . ' Screamy breath, deeper. And still grinning, as if they share some horrible secret. Do they? 'So . . . don't . . . insult my . . . intelligence. Or . . . your own.'

Yes. She knows. *It.* The long boy, he calls it. Or just the thing. Or sometimes the thing with the endless piebald side. Once she meant to look up *piebald* in the dictionary – she is not bright about words, not like Scott is – she really did, but then she got sidetracked. And actually, it's more than just a few times he's spoken of that thing. Especially just lately. He says you can see it if you look through dirty water glasses. If you look through them just the right way, and in the hours after midnight.

He lets go of her, or maybe just loses the strength to hold on. Lisey pulls back a little – not far. His eyes regard her from their deep and blackened sockets. They are as brilliant as ever – as aware, as full of pain – but she sees they are also full of terror and (this is what frightens her the most) some wretched amusement. As if what's happened to him is in some way *funny*.

Still speaking low – perhaps so only she can hear, maybe because it's the best he can manage, probably both – Scott says, 'Listen. Listen, Lisey. I'll make how it sounds when it looks around.'

'Scott, no – you have to stop.'

He pays no attention. He draws in another of those screaming lung-shot breaths, then purses his wet red lips in a tight O, as if to whistle. Instead of whistling he makes a low, indescribably nasty *chuffing* noise that drives a spray of blood up his clenched throat, through his lips, and into the sweltering air. A girl sees this gusher of fine ruby droplets and cries out in revulsion. This time the crowd doesn't need the voice of authority to tell them to move back; they do so on their own, leaving the three of them – Lisey, Scott, and the cop – a perimeter of at least four feet all the way around.

The sound – dear God, it *is* a kind of grunting – is mercifully short. Scott coughs, his chest heaving, the wound spilling more blood in rhythmic pulses, then beckons her back down with one finger. She comes, leaning on her burning hands. His socketed eyes compel her; his mortal grin compels her.

He turns his head to the side, spits a wad of blood onto the hot tar. Then he turns back to her. 'I . . . could . . . call it that way,' he whispers. 'It would come. You'd . . . be . . . rid of me. My everlasting . . . quack.'

She understands he means it, and for a moment (surely it is the power of his eyes) she believes it's true. He will make the sound again, only a little louder this time, and somewhere the long boy – that lord of sleepless nights – will turn its unspeakable hungry head. A moment later, in this world, Scott Landon will simply shiver on the pavement and die. The death certificate will say something sane, but she will know. His dark thing finally saw him and came for him and ate him alive.

So now come the things they will never speak of later, not to others nor between themselves. Too awful. Each long marriage has two hearts, one light and one dark. This is the dark heart of theirs, the one mad true secret. She will ponder it that night in the terrible moonlight while the dogs bark. Now she leans close to him on the baking pavement, sure he is dying, nonetheless determined to hold onto him if she can. If it means fighting the long boy for him – with nothing but her fingernails, come it to that – she will.

'Well . . . Lisey? What . . . do . . . you . . . say?'

Leaning even closer. Leaning into the shivering heat of him, the sweat- and blood-stink of him. Leaning in until she can smell the last palest ghost of the Foamy he shaved with that morning and the Prell he shampooed with. Leaning in until her lips touch his ear. She whispers: 'Be quiet, Scott. Just be quiet.' She pauses, then adds, louder – loud enough to make him jerk his head on the pavement: *'Leave that fucking thing alone and it will go away.'*

When she looks at him again, his eyes are different – saner, somehow, but also weaker. 'Have . . . you seen . . . ? Do . . . you know . . . ?'

'I know *you*,' she says. 'Don't you ever make that noise again.'

He licks at his lips. She sees the blood on his tongue and it turns her stomach, but she doesn't pull away from him.

'I'm so hot,' he says. 'If only I had a piece of ice to suck . . .'

'Soon,' Lisey says, not knowing if she's promising rashly and not caring. 'I'm getting it for you.' At last she can hear the ambulance howling its way toward them. That's something. Yet she is still in her heart convinced it will be too late. That sound he made, that *chuffing* sound, has almost shot her nerve.

And then, a kind of miracle. The girl with the bows on

her shoulders and the new scrapes on her palms fights her way through to the front of the crowd. She is gasping like someone who has just run a race and sweat coats her cheeks and neck . . . but she's holding two big waxed paper cups in her hands. 'I spilled half the shitting Cokes getting back here,' she says, throwing a brief, baleful backward glance at the crowd, 'but I got the ice okay. Ice is ni – ' Then her eyes roll up almost to the whites and she reels backward, all loosy-goosey in her sneakers. The campus cop – bless him, oh bless him with many blessings, huh-yooge batch of orifice and all – grabs her, steadies her, and takes one of the cups. He hands it down to Lisey, then urges the other Lisa, coed Lisa, to drink from the remaining cup. Lisey Landon pays no attention. Later, replaying all this, she'll be a little in awe of her own single-mindedness. Now she only thinks, *Just keep her from falling on top of me again if she faints*, and turns back to Scott.

He's shivering worse than ever, and his eyes are dulling out. And still he tries. 'Lisey . . . so hot . . . ice . . . '

'I have it, Scott. Now will you for once just shut your everlasting mouth?'

And for a wonder, he does. A Scott Landon first. *Maybe*, she thinks, *he's just out of wind*.

Lisey drives her hand deep into the cup, sending Coke all the way to the top and splooshing over the edge. The cold is shocking and utterly wonderful. She clutches a good handful of ice chips, thinking how ironic this is: whenever she and Scott stop at a turnpike rest area and she uses a machine that dispenses cups of soda instead of cans or bottles, she always hammers on the NO ICE button, feeling righteous – others may allow the evil soft-drink companies to shortchange them by dispensing half a cup of ice and half a cup of soda, but not Lisa Landon! What was

Good Ma Debusher's saying? *I didn't fall off a hay truck yesterday!*

His eyes are half-closed now, but he opens his mouth and when she first rubs his lips with her handful of ice and then pops one of the melting shards on to his bloody tongue, his shivering suddenly stops. God, it's magic. Emboldened, she rubs her freezing, leaking hand along his right cheek, his left cheek, and then across his fore-head, where drops of Coke-colored water drip into his eyebrows.

'Oh, Lisey, that's heaven,' he says, and although still screamy, his voice sounds more rational to her . . . more with-it, more *there*. The ambulance has pulled up on the left side of the crowd and she can hear an impatient male voice shouting, *'Paramedics! Let us through! Paramedics! C'mon, people, let us through!'*

'Lisey,' he whispers.

'Scott, you need to be quiet.'

But he means to have his say; as always, and until death closes his mouth sixteen years later, Scott Landon will have his say.

'Take . . . a motel room . . . close to . . . hospital.'

'You don't need to tell me th – '

He gives her hand an impatient squeeze, stopping her. 'It may . . . have heard you . . . *seen* you.'

'Scott, I don't know what you're – '

The paramedics come shouldering through the crowd. She and Scott are down to only seconds now, and Scott knows it. He looks at her urgently.

'First thing . . . you do . . . water glasses . . . '

He can say no more. Luckily, he doesn't need to.

VI

After checking in at the Greenview Motel and before walking to the hospital half a mile away to visit her husband, Lisey Landon goes into the bathroom. There are two glasses on the shelf over the sink, and they are the real kind, not plastic. She puts both of them in her purse, careful not to look at either one as she does so. On her walk to the hospital she takes them out one at a time, still not looking at them, and throws them into the gutter. The sound of them breaking comforts her even more than the sound of the little shovel's scoop, connecting first with the pistol and then with Blondie's face.

FRIENDS, LOVERS, CHOCOLATE
Alexander McCall Smith

The man in the brown Harris tweed overcoat – a double-breasted overcoat with three small leather-covered buttons on the cuffs – made his way slowly down the street that led down the spine of Edinburgh. He was aware of the sea-gulls which had drifted in from the shore and which were swooping down on to the cobblestones, picking up dropped fragments from somebody who had been careless with a fish. Their mews were the loudest sound in the street at that moment, as there was little traffic and the city was unusually quiet. It was October, it was mid-morning, and there were few people about. A boy on the other side of the road, scruffy and tousle-haired, was leading a dog along with a makeshift leash – a length of string. The dog, a small Scottish terrier, seemed unwilling to follow the boy and glanced for a moment at the man as if imploring him to intervene to stop the tugging and the pulling. There must be a saint for such dogs, thought the man; a saint for such dogs in their small prisons.

The man reached the St Mary's Street crossroads. On the corner on his right was a pub, the World's End, a place of resort for fiddlers and singers; on his left, Jeffrey Street curved round and dipped under the great arch of the North Bridge. Through the gap in the buildings, he could see the flags on top of the Balmoral Hotel, the blue and white cross of the Saltire, the Scottish flag, the familiar diagonal stripes of the Union Jack. There was a stiff breeze from the North, from Fife, which made the flags stand out from their poles with pride, like the flags on the prow of a ship ploughing into the wind. And that, he thought, was what Scotland was like: a small vessel pointed out to sea, a small vessel buffeted by the wind.

He crossed the street and continued down the hill. He walked past a fishmonger, with its gilt fish-sign suspended over the street, and the entrance to a close, one of those small stone passages that ran off the street underneath the tenements. And then he was where he wanted to be, out-side the Canongate Kirk, the high-gabled church set just a few paces off the High Street. At the top of the gable, stark against the light blue of the sky, the arms of the Kirk, a stag's antlers, gilded, spiky, against the background of a raised cross.

He entered the gate and looked up. One might be in Holland, he thought, with that gable; but there were too many reminders of Scotland – the wind, the sky, the grey stone. And there was what he had come to see, the stone which he visited every year on this day, this day when the poet had died at the age of twenty four. He walked across the grass towards the stone, its shape reflecting the gable of the kirk, its lettering still clear after two hundred years. Robert Burns himself had paid for this stone to be erected, in homage to his brother in the muse, and had written the lines of its inscription: *This simple stone directs Pale Scotia's way / To pour her sorrows o'er her poet's dust*.

He stood quite still. There were others who could be visited here. Adam Smith, who conjured up economics, had his stone here, more impressive than this, more ornate; but this was the one that made one weep.

He reached into a pocket of his overcoat and took out a small black notebook of the sort that used to advertise itself as waterproof. Opening it, he read the lines that he had written out himself, copied from a collection of Robert Garioch's poems. He read aloud, but in a low voice although there was nobody present save for him and the dead:

> Canongait kirkyaird in the failing year
> Is auld and grey, the wee roseirs are bare,
> Five gulls leem white agin the dirty air
> Why are they here? There's naething for them here
> Why are we here oursels?

Yes, he thought. Why am I here myself? Because I admired this man, this Robert Fergusson, who wrote such beautiful words in the few years given him, and because at least somebody should remember and come here on this day each year. And this, he told himself, was the last time that he would be able to do this. This was his final visit. If their predictions were correct, and unless something turned up, which he thought was unlikely, this was the last of his pilgrimages.

He looked down at his notebook again. He began to read them out. The chiselled Scots words were taken up by the wind and carried away.

> Strang, present dool
> Ruggs at my hairt. Lichtlie this gin ye daur:
> Here Robert Burns knelt and kissed the mool.

Strong, present sorrow
Tugs at my heart. Treat this lightly if you dare:
Here Robert Burns knelt and kissed the soil.

He took a step back. There was nobody there to observe the tears which had come to his eyes, but he wiped them away in embarrassment. *Strang, present dool.* Yes. And then he nodded towards the stone and turned round, and that was when the woman came running up the path towards him. He saw her almost trip as the heel of a shoe caught in a crack between two paving stones, and he cried out. But she recovered herself and came on towards him, waving her hands.

'Ian. Ian.' She was breathless. And he knew immediately what news she had brought him, and he looked at her gravely. She said, 'Yes.' And then she smiled, and leant forward to embrace him.

'When?' he asked, stuffing the notebook back into his pocket.

'Right away,' she said. 'Now. Right now. They'll take you down there straight away.'

They began to walk back along the path, away from the stone. He had been warned not to run, and could not, as he would rapidly become breathless. But he could walk quite fast on the flat, and they were soon back at the gate to the kirk where the black taxi was waiting, ready to take them.

'Whatever happens,' he said as they climbed into the taxi. 'Come back to this place for me. It's the one thing I do every year. On this day.'

'You'll be back next year,' she said, reaching out to take his hand.

*

On the other side of Edinburgh, in another season, Cat stood at Isabel Dalhousie's front door, her finger poised by the bell. She gazed at the stonework. She noticed that in parts the discoloration of the stone was becoming more pronounced, and that in certain lights, and at certain times, such as that evening, the house would not have been out of place altogether elsewhere; in France, for example, on the edge of a prosperous provincial town; or in Italy, as a villa on the rich, misty Emilian plains. She looked at the triangular gable above her aunt's bedroom window; the stone was flaking slightly, and a patch had fallen off here and there, like a ripened scab, exposing fresh skin below. This slow decline had its own charms; a house, like anything else, should not be denied the dignity of natural ageing; within reason, of course.

For the most part, the house was in good order; a discreet and sympathetic house, in spite of its size. And it was known, too, for its hospitality. Everyone who called there – irrespective of their mission – would be courteously received and offered, if the time were appropriate, a glass of dry white wine in spring and summer, and red in autumn and winter. They would then be listened to, again with courtesy; for Isabel believed in giving moral attention to everyone. This made her profoundly egalitarian, not in the non-discriminating sense of most contemporary egalitarians, who sometimes ignore the real moral differences between people (the good and the evil are *not* the same, Isabel would say). If we are all moral equals, then should we not perhaps all be judged by the same standards? Isabel thought that we should, and this meant that she felt uncomfortable with moral relativists and their penchant for non-judgementalism. But of course we must be judgemental, she said, *when there is something to be judged.*

Isabel had studied philosophy and had a part-time job as general editor of the *Review of Applied Ethics*. It was not a demanding job in terms of the time it required, and it was badly-paid; in fact, at Isabel's own suggestion, rising production costs had been partly offset by a cut in her own salary. Not that payment mattered; her share of the Louisiana Land and Resources Company, left her by her mother – her sainted American mother, as she called her – provided more than she could possibly need. Isabel was, in fact, wealthy, although that was a word which she did not like to use, especially of herself. She was indifferent to material wealth, although she was attentive to what she described, with characteristic modesty, as her minor projects of giving (they were actually very generous).

'And what are these projects?' Cat had once asked.

Isabel looked embarrassed. 'Charitable ones, I suppose. Or eleemosynary if you prefer long words. Nice word that – eleemosynary. But I don't normally talk about it.'

Cat frowned. There were things about her aunt that puzzled her. If one gave to charity, then why not mention it?

'One must be discreet,' Isabel continued. She was not one for circumlocution, but she believed that one should never refer to the one's own good works. A good work, once drawn attention to by its author, inevitably became an exercise in self-congratulation. That was what was wrong with the lists of names of donors in the opera programmes. Would they have given if their generosity was not going to be recorded in the programme? Isabel thought that in many cases they would not. But of course if the only way one could raise money for the arts was through appealing to vanity, then it was probably worth doing. But her own name never appeared in such lists, a fact which had not gone unnoticed in Edinburgh.

'She's mean,' whispered some. 'Rich as Croesus, but mean.'

They were wrong, of course, as the uncharitable so often are. In one year, Isabel, unrecorded by name in any programme, had given eight thousand pounds to the Scottish Opera: three thousand towards a production of *Hansel and Gretel*, and five thousand to help secure a fine Italian tenor for a *Cavalleria Rusticana* performed in the ill-fitting costumes of 1930s Italy, complete with brown-shirted *Fascisti* in the chorus.

'Such fine singing from your *Fascisti*,' Isabel had remarked at the party which followed the production.

'They love to dress up as fascists,' the chorus-master had responded. 'Something to do with only being in the chorus, I suspect.'

This remark had been greeted with silence. Some of the *Fascisti* had overheard the remark.

'Only in the most attenuated way,' the chorus-master had added, looking into his glass of wine. 'But then again, perhaps not. Perhaps not.'

'Money,' said Cat. 'That's the problem. Money.'

Isabel handed Cat a glass of wine. 'It inevitably is,' she said.

'Yes,' Cat went on. 'I suppose that if I were prepared to offer enough I would be able to get somebody suitable to stand in for me. But I can't. I have to run it as a business, and I can't make a loss.'

Isabel nodded. Cat owned a delicatessen just a few streets away, in Bruntsfield, and although it was successful, she knew that the line between profitability and failure was a narrow one. As it was, she had one full-time employee to pay, Eddie, a young man who seemed to be on the verge of tears much of the time, haunted, thought Isabel, by something which Cat could not, or would not, speak about. Eddie could be left in control for short periods, but not for a week it seemed.

'He panics,' said Cat. 'It gets too much for him and he panics.'

Cat had been invited to a wedding in Italy and wanted to go with a party of friends. They would attend the wedding in Messina and then move north to a house which they had rented for a week in Umbria. The time of year was ideal; the weather would be perfect.

'I have to go,' said Cat. 'I just have to.'

Isabel smiled. Cat would never ask outright for a favour, but her intention was transparent. 'I suppose . . . ' she began. 'I suppose I could do it again. I rather enjoyed it last time. And if you remember, I made more than you usually do. The takings went up.'

This amused Cat. 'You probably overcharged,' she said. And then a pause, before she continued, 'I didn't raise the issue to get you to . . . I wouldn't want to force you.'

'Of course not,' said Isabel.

'But it would make all the difference,' Cat went on quickly. 'You know how everything works. And Eddie likes you.'

Isabel was surprised. Did Eddie have a view on her? He hardly ever spoke to her, and certainly never smiled. But the thought that he liked her made her warm towards him. Perhaps he might confide in her, as he had confided in Cat, and she would be able to help him in some way. Or she could put him in touch with somebody: there were people who could help in such circumstances; she could pay for it if necessary.

They discussed the details. Cat would be leaving in ten days' time. If Isabel came for a handover day before then, she could be shown the current stock and the order book. Consignments of wine and salamis were expected while Cat was away and these would have to be attended to. And then there was the whole issue of making sure that the surfaces were cleaned; a fussy procedure subject to an entire litany of regulations. Eddie, however, knew all about that; but you had to watch him; he was funny about olives and often put them in containers marked down for coleslaw.

'It will be far more difficult than editing the *Review of Applied Ethics*,' said Cat, smiling. 'Far more difficult.'

Which might have been true, thought Isabel, although she did not say it. Editing a journal was largely repetitive work; sending letters to reviewers and assessors; discussing deadlines with copy-editors and printers. All that was mundane work; reading the papers and dealing with authors was a different matter. That required insight and a large measure of tact. In her experience, the authors of papers which were turned down almost inevitably proved resentful. And the more incompetent or eccentric the paper – and there were many of those – the more truculent the disappointed authors became. One such author – or his paper – lay on her desk even now. 'The Rightness of Vice'. A title which reminded her of a recent book she had reviewed: *In Praise of Sin*. But while *In Praise of Sin* had been a serious investigation of the limits of moralism – and ultimately claimed to be in favour of virtue – 'The Rightness of Vice' had no truck with virtue. It was about the alleged benefits for character of vice, provided that the vice in question was what a person really wanted to do. That was defensible – just – thought Isabel, provided that the vice was a tolerable one (drinking, gluttony and so on) but how could one possibly argue in favour of the sort of vices which the author of the paper had in mind. It was impossible, thought Isabel. Who could defend . . . she went over in her mind some of the vices explored by the author, but stopped. Even by their Latin names, these vices barely bore thinking about. Did people really do *that*? The answer, she supposed, was that they did, but she very much doubted that they would expect a philosopher to spring to their defence. And yet here was an Australian professor of philosophy doing just that. Well, she had a responsibility to her readers. She could not defend the indefensible. She would send the article back with a short note, something like: *Dear Professor Curtis, I'm so sorry, but we just can't. People feel very strongly about these things, you know. And they would blame me for what you say. They really would. Yours sincerely, Isabel Dalhousie.*

Isabel put thought of vice behind her and turned her attention back to Cat. 'It may be difficult,' she said. 'But I think I'll manage.'

'You can say no,' said Cat.

'Can, but shall not,' said Isabel. 'You go to the wedding.'

Cat smiled. 'I'll reciprocate some day,' she said. 'I'll be you for a few weeks and you can go away.'

'You could never be me,' said Isabel. 'And I could never be you. We never know enough about another person to be them. We think we do, but we can never be sure.'

'You know what I mean,' said Cat. 'I'll come and live here and reply to your letters and so on while you get away.'

Isabel nodded. 'I'll bear that in mind. But there's no need to think of reciprocation. I suspect that I shall enjoy myself.'

'You will,' said Cat. 'You'll enjoy the customers – or some of them.'

Cat stayed, and they ate a light supper in the garden room,

enjoying the last of the evening sun. It was June – close to the solstice – and it never became truly dark in Edinburgh, even at midnight. The summer had been slow to come, but had now arrived and the days were long and warm.

'I've been feeling lazy in this weather,' Isabel remarked to Cat. 'Working in your shop is exactly what I need to wake me up.'

'And Italy is exactly what I need to wind me down,' said Cat. 'Not that the wedding itself should be quiet – anything but.'

Isabel asked who was getting married. She knew few of Cat's friends, and tended to get them mixed up. There were too many Kirstys and Craigs, Isabel thought; they had become interchangeable in her mind.

'Kirsty,' said Cat. 'You've met her with me once or twice, I think.'

'Oh,' said Isabel. 'Kirsty.'

'She met an Italian last year when she was teaching English in Catania. Salvatore. They fell for one another and that was it.'

For a moment Isabel was silent. She had fallen for John Liamor, and that had been it too. But all these Kirstys were so sensible; they would not make a bad choice.

'What does he do?' Isabel asked. She half-expected Cat not to know; it always surprised her that Cat seemed uninterested in, or unaware of, what people did. For Isabel it was fundamentally important information if one were even to begin to understand somebody.

Cat smiled. 'Kirsty doesn't really know,' she said. 'I know that'll surprise you, but she says that whenever she's asked Salvatore he's become evasive. He says that he's some sort of businessman who works for his father. But she can't find out exactly what this business is.'

Isabel stared at Cat. It was clear to her – immediately clear – what Salvatore's father did.

'And she doesn't care,' Isabel ventured. 'She's still prepared to marry him?'

'Why not?' said Cat. 'Just because you don't know what happens in somebody's office doesn't mean that you shouldn't marry them.'

'But what if this . . . this office is headquarters of a protection racket? What then?'

Cat laughed. 'A protection racket? Don't be ridiculous. There's nothing to suggest that it's a protection racket.'

Isabel thought that any accusations of ridiculousness were being made in exactly the wrong direction.

'Cat,' she said quietly. 'It's Italy. In the South of Italy if you won't disclose what you do, then it means one thing. Organised crime. That's just the way it is. And the most common form of organised crime is the protection racket.'

Cat stared at her aunt. 'Nonsense,' she said. 'You have an overheated imagination.'

'And Kirsty's is distinctly under-heated,' retorted Isabel. 'I simply can't imagine marrying somebody who would hide that sort of thing from me. I couldn't marry a gangster.'

'Salvatore's not a gangster,' said Cat. 'He's nice. I've met him several times and I like him.'

Isabel looked at the floor. The fact that Cat could say this merely emphasised her inability to tell good men from bad. This Kirsty was in for a rude awakening, with her handsome young *mafioso* husband. He would want a compliant, unquestioning wife, who would look the other way when it came to his dealings with his cronies. A Scotswoman was unlikely to understand this; she would expect equality and consideration, which this Salvatore would not give her once they were married. It was a disaster in the making and Isabel thought that Cat simply could not see it, as she had been unable to see through Toby, her previous boyfriend; he of the Lladró porcelain looks and the tendency to wear crushed strawberry corduroy trousers. Perhaps she would come back from Italy with an Italian of her own. Now that would be interesting.

SATURDAY
Ian McEwan

1

Some hours before dawn Henry Perowne, a neurosurgeon, wakes to find himself already in motion, pushing back the covers from a sitting position, and then rising to his feet. It's not clear to him when exactly he became conscious, nor does it seem relevant. He's never done such a thing before, but he isn't alarmed or even faintly surprised, for the movement is easy, and pleasurable in his limbs, and his back and legs feel unusually strong. He stands there, naked by the bed – he always sleeps naked – feeling his full height, aware of his wife's patient breathing and of the wintry bedroom air on his skin. That too is a pleasurable sensation. His bedside clock shows three forty. He has no idea what he's doing out of bed: he has no need to relieve himself, nor is he disturbed by a dream or some element of the day before, or even by the state of the world. It's as if, standing there in the darkness, he's materialised out of nothing, fully formed, unencumbered.

He doesn't feel tired, despite the hour or his recent labours, nor is his conscience troubled by any recent case.

189

In fact, he's alert and empty-headed and inexplicably elated. With no decision made, no motivation at all, he begins to move towards the nearest of the three bedroom windows and experiences such ease and lightness in his tread that he suspects at once he's dreaming or sleepwalking. If it is the case, he'll be disappointed. Dreams don't interest him; that this should be real is a richer possibility. And he's entirely himself, he is certain of it, and he knows that sleep is behind him: to know the difference between it and waking, to know the boundaries, is the essence of sanity.

The bedroom is large and uncluttered. As he glides across it with almost comic facility, the prospect of the experience ending saddens him briefly, then the thought is gone. He is by the centre window, pulling back the tall folding wooden shutters with care so as not to wake Rosalind. In this he's selfish as well as solicitous. He doesn't wish to be asked what he's about – what answer could he give, and why relinquish this moment in the attempt? He opens the second shutter, letting it concertina into the casement, and quietly raises the sash window. It is many feet taller than him, but it slides easily upwards, hoisted by its concealed lead counterweight.

His skin tightens as the February air pours in around him, but he isn't troubled by the cold. From the second floor he faces the night, the city in its icy white light, the skeletal trees in the square, and thirty feet below, the black arrowhead railings like a row of spears. There's a degree or two of frost and the air is clear. The streetlamp glare hasn't quite obliterated all the stars; above the Regency façade on the other side of the square hang remnants of constellations in the southern sky. That particular façade is a reconstruction, a pastiche – wartime Fitzrovia took some hits from the Luftwaffe – and right behind is the Post

Office Tower, municipal and seedy by day, but at night, half-concealed and decently illuminated, a valiant memorial to more optimistic days.

And now, what days are these? Baffled and fearful, he mostly thinks when he takes time from his weekly round to consider. But he doesn't feel that now. He leans forwards, pressing his weight onto his palms against the sill, exulting in the emptiness and clarity of the scene. His vision – always good – seems to have sharpened. He sees the paving stone mica glistening in the pedestrianised square, pigeon excrement hardened by distance and cold into something almost beautiful, like a scattering of snow. He likes the symmetry of black cast-iron posts and their even darker shadows, and the lattice of cobbled gutters. The overfull litter baskets suggest abundance rather than squalor; the vacant benches set around the circular gardens look benignly expectant of their daily traffic – cheerful lunchtime office crowds, the solemn, studious boys from the Indian hostel, lovers in quiet raptures or crisis, the crepuscular drug dealers, the ruined old lady with her wild, haunting calls. Go away! she'll shout for hours at a time, and squawk harshly, sounding like some marsh bird or zoo creature.

Standing here, as immune to the cold as a marble statue, gazing towards Charlotte Street, towards a foreshortened jumble of façades, scaffolding and pitched roofs, Henry thinks the city is a success, a brilliant invention, a biological masterpiece – millions teeming around the accumulated and layered achievements of the centuries, as though around a coral reef, sleeping, working, entertaining themselves, harmonious for the most part, nearly everyone wanting it to work. And the Perownes' own corner, a triumph of congruent proportion; the perfect square laid out by Robert Adam enclosing a perfect circle of garden – an eighteenth-century dream bathed and embraced by modernity, by street light from above, and from below by fibre-optic cables, and cool fresh water coursing down pipes, and sewage borne away in an instant of forgetting.

An habitual observer of his own moods, he wonders about this sustained, distorting euphoria. Perhaps down at the molecular level there's been a chemical accident while he slept – something like a spilled tray of drinks, prompting dopamine-like receptors to initiate a kindly cascade of intracellular events; or it's the prospect of a Saturday, or the paradoxical consequence of extreme tiredness. It's true, he finished the week in a state of unusual depletion. He came home to an empty house, and lay in the bath with a book, content to be talking to no one. It was his literate, too literate daughter Daisy who sent the biography of Darwin which in turn has something to do with a Conrad novel she wants him to read and which he has yet to start – seafaring, however morally fraught, doesn't much interest him. For some years now she's been addressing what she believes is his astounding ignorance, guiding his literary education, scolding him for poor taste and insensitivity. She has a point – straight from school to medical school to the slavish hours of a junior doctor, then the total absorption of neurosurgery training spliced with committed fatherhood – for fifteen years he barely touched a non-medical book at all. On the other hand, he thinks he's seen enough death, fear, courage and suffering to supply half a dozen literatures. Still, he submits to her reading lists – they're his means of remaining in touch as she grows away from her family into unknowable womanhood in a suburb of Paris; tonight she'll be home for the first time in six months – another cause for euphoria.

He was behind with his assignments from Daisy. With one toe occasionally controlling a fresh input of hot water, he blearily read an account of Darwin's dash to complete *The Origin of Species*, and a summary of the concluding pages, amended in later editions. At the same time he was listening to the radio news. The stolid Mr Blix has been addressing the UN again – there's a general impression that he's rather undermined the case for war. Then, certain he'd taken in nothing at all, Perowne switched the radio off, turned back the pages and read again. At times this biography made him comfortably nostalgic for a verdant, horse-drawn, affectionate England; at others he was faintly depressed by the way a whole life could be contained by a few hundred pages – bottled, like homemade chutney. And by how easily an existence, its ambitions, networks of family and friends, all its cherished stuff, solidly possessed, could so entirely vanish.

Afterwards, he stretched out on the bed to consider his supper, and remembered nothing more. Rosalind must have drawn the covers over him when she came in from work. She would have kissed him. Forty-eight years old, profoundly asleep at nine thirty on a Friday night – this is modern professional life. He works hard, everyone around him works hard, and this week he's been pushed harder by a flu outbreak among the hospital staff – his operating list has been twice the usual length.

By means of balancing and doubling, he was able to perform major surgery in one theatre, supervise a senior registrar in another, and perform minor procedures in a third. He has two neurosurgical registrars in his firm at present – Sally Madden who is almost qualified and entirely reliable, and a year-two registrar, Rodney Browne from Guyana, gifted, hardworking, but still unsure of himself. Perowne's consultant anaesthetist, Jay Strauss, has his own registrar, Gita Syal.

For three days, keeping Rodney at his side, Perowne moved between the three suites – the sound of his own clogs on the corridor's polished floors and the various squeaks and groans of the theatre swing doors sounded like orchestral accompaniments.

Friday's list was typical. While Sally closed up a patient Perowne went next door to relieve an elderly lady of her trigeminal neuralgia, her tic douloureux. These minor operations can still give him pleasure – he likes to be fast and accurate. He slipped a gloved forefinger into the back of her mouth to feel the route, then, with barely a glance at the image intensifier, slid a long needle through the outside of her cheek, all the way up to the trigeminal ganglion. Jay came in from next door to watch Gita bringing the lady to brief consciousness. Electrical stimulation of the needle's tip caused a tingling in her face, and once she'd drowsily confirmed the position was correct – Perowne had it right first time – she was put down again while the nerve was 'cooked' by radiofrequency thermocoagulation. The delicate trick was to eliminate her pain while leaving her an awareness of light touch – all done in fifteen minutes; three years' misery, of sharp, stabbing pain, ended.

He clipped the neck of a middle cerebral artery aneurysm – he's something of a master in the art – and performed a biopsy for a tumour in the thalamus, a region where it's not possible to operate. The patient was a twenty-eight-year-old professional tennis player, already suffering acute memory loss. As Perowne drew the needle clear from the depths of the brain he could see at a glance that the tissue was abnormal. He held out little hope for radio- or chemotherapy. Confirmation came in a verbal report from the lab, and that afternoon he broke the news to the young man's elderly parents.

The next case was a craniotomy for a meningioma in a fifty-three-year-old woman, a primary school head-mistress. The tumour sat above the motor strip and was sharply defined, rolling away neatly before the probing of his Rhoton dissector – an entirely curative process. Sally closed that one up while Perowne went next door to carry out a multi-level lumbar laminectomy on an obese forty-four-year-old man, a gardener who worked in Hyde Park. He cut through four inches of subcutaneous fat before the vertebrae were exposed, and the man wobbled unhelpfully on the table whenever Perowne exerted downwards pres-sure to clip away at the bone.

For an old friend, a specialist in Ear, Nose and Throat, Perowne opened up an acoustic in a seventeen-year-old boy – it's odd how these ENT people shy away from making their own difficult routes in. Perowne made a large, rectan-gular bone flap behind the ear, which took well over an hour, irritating Jay Strauss who was wanting to get on with the firm's own list. Finally the tumour lay exposed to the operating microscope – a small vestibular schwannoma lying barely three millimetres from the cochlea. Leaving his specialist friend to perform the excision, Perowne hurried out to a second minor procedure which in turn caused him some irritation – a loud young woman with an habitually aggrieved manner wanted her spinal stimulator moved from back to front. Only the month before he had shifted it round after she complained that it was uncomfortable to sit down. Now she was saying the stimulator made it impossible to lie in bed. He made a long incision across her abdomen and wasted valuable time, up to his elbows inside her, searching for the battery wire. He was sure she'd be back before long.

For lunch he had a factory-wrapped tuna and cucumber sandwich with a bottle of mineral water. In the cramped coffee room whose toast and microwaved pasta always remind him of the odours of major surgery, he sat next to Heather, the much-loved Cockney lady who helps clean the theatres between procedures. She gave him an account of her son-inlaw's arrest for armed robbery after being mistakenly picked out of a police line-up. But his alibi was perfect – at the time of the crime he was at the dentist's having a wisdom tooth removed. Elsewhere in the room, the talk was of the flu epidemic – one of the scrub nurses and a trainee Operating Department Practitioner working for Jay Strauss were sent home that morning. After fifteen minutes Perowne took his firm back to work. While Sally was next door drilling a hole in the skull of an old man, a retired traffic warden, to relieve the pressure of his internal bleeding – a chronic subdural haematoma – Perowne used the theatre's latest piece of equipment, a computerised image-guidance system, to help him with a craniotomy for a resection of a right posterior frontal glioma. Then he let Rodney take the lead in another burr hole for a chronic subdural.

The culmination of today's list was the removal of a pilocytic astrocytoma from a fourteen-year-old Nigerian girl who lives in Brixton with her aunt and uncle, a Church of England vicar. The tumour was best reached through the back of the head, by an infratentorial supracerebellar route, with the anaesthetised patient in a sitting position. This in turn created special problems for Jay Strauss, for there was a possibility of air entering a vein and causing an embolism. Andrea Chapman was a problem patient, a problem niece. She arrived in England at the age of twelve – the dismayed vicar and his wife showed Perowne the photograph – a scrubbed girl in a frock and tight ribbons with a shy smile.

Something in her that village life in rural north Nigeria kept buttoned down was released once she started at her local Brixton comprehensive. She took to the music, the clothes, the talk, the values – the street. She had attitude, the vicar confided while his wife was trying to settle Andrea on the ward. His niece took drugs, got drunk, shoplifted, bunked off school, hated authority, and 'swore like a merchant seaman'. Could it be the tumour was pressing down on some part of her brain?

Perowne could offer no such comfort. The tumour was remote from the frontal lobes. It was deep in the superior cerebellar vermis. She'd already suffered early-morning headaches, blind spots and ataxia – unsteadiness. These symptoms failed to dispel her suspicion that her condition was part of a plot – the hospital, in league with her guardians, the school, the police – to curb her nights in the clubs. Within hours of being admitted she was in conflict with the nurses, the ward sister and an elderly patient who said she wouldn't tolerate the obscene language. Perowne had his own difficulties talking her through the ordeals that lay ahead. Even when Andrea wasn't aroused, she affected to talk like a rapper on MTV, swaying her upper body as she sat up in bed, making circular movements with her palms downwards, soothing the air in front of her, in preparation for one of her own storms. But he admired her spirit, and the fierce dark eyes, the perfect teeth, and the clean pink tongue lashing itself round the words it formed. She smiled joyously, even when she was shouting in apparent fury, as though she was tickled by just how much she could get away with. It took Jay Strauss, an American with the warmth and directness that no one else in this English hospital could muster, to bring her into line.

Andrea's operation lasted five hours and went well. She was placed in a sitting position, with her head-clamp bolted to a frame in front of her. Opening up the back of the head needed great care because of the vessels running close under the bone. Rodney leaned in at Perowne's side to irrigate the drilling and cauterise the bleeding with the bipolar. Finally it lay exposed, the tentorium – the tent – a pale delicate structure of beauty, like the little whirl of a veiled dancer, where the dura is gathered and parted again. Below it lay the cerebellum. By cutting away carefully, Perowne allowed gravity itself to draw the cerebellum down – no need for retractors – and it was possible to see deep into the region where the pineal lay, with the tumour extending in a vast red mass right in front of it. The astrocytoma was well defined and had only partially infiltrated surrounding tissue. Perowne was able to excise almost all of it without damaging any eloquent region. He allowed Rodney several minutes with the microscope and the sucker, and let him do the closing up. Perowne did the head dressing himself, and when he finally came away from the theatres, he wasn't feeling tired at all. Operating never wearies him – once busy within the enclosed world of his firm, the theatre and its ordered procedures, and absorbed by the vivid foreshortening of the operating microscope as he follows a corridor to a desired site, he experiences a superhuman capacity, more like a craving, for work. As for the rest of the week, the two morning clinics made no more demand than usual. He's too experienced to be touched by the varieties of distress he encounters – his obligation is to be useful. Nor did the ward rounds or the various weekly committees tire him. It was the paperwork on Friday afternoon that brought him down, the backlog of referrals, and responses to referrals, abstracts for two conferences, letters to colleagues and editors, an unfinished peer review, contributions to management initiatives, and government changes to the structure of the Trust, and yet more revisions to teaching practices. There's to be a new look – there's always a new look – at the hospital's Emergency Plan.

Simple train crashes are no longer all that are envisaged, and words like 'catastrophe' and 'mass fatalities', 'chemical and biological warfare' and 'major attack' have recently become bland through repetition. In the past year he's become aware of new committees and subcommittees spawning, and lines of command that stretch up and out of the hospital, beyond the medical hierarchies, up through the distant reaches of the Civil Service to the Home Secretary's office.

Perowne dictated monotonously, and long after his secretary went home he typed in his overheated box of an office on the hospital's third floor. What dragged him back was an unfamiliar lack of fluency. He prides himself on speed and a sleek, wry style. It never needs much forethought – typing and composing are one. Now he was stumbling. And though the professional jargon didn't desert him – it's second nature – his prose accumulated awkwardly. Individual words brought to mind unwieldy objects – bicycles, deckchairs, coat hangers – strewn across his path. He composed a sentence in his head, then lost it on the page, or typed himself into a grammatical cul-de-sac and had to sweat his way out. Whether this debility was the cause or the consequence of fatigue he didn't pause to consider. He was stubborn and he pushed himself to the end. At eight in the evening he concluded the last in a series of e-mails, and stood up from his desk where he had been hunched since four. On his way out he looked in at his patients in the ICU. There were no problems, and Andrea was doing fine – she was sleeping and all her signs were good. Less than half an hour later he was back home, in his bath, and soon after, he too was asleep.

EARTH AND SKY
Vikram Seth

How shall I know where I should go?
How may I see the I that's me?

The earth so high, the sky so low –
How may I see where I must go?
The dust so wet, the rain so dry –
How shall I know the me that's I?

By note and word and thought and fact
I plan, I shape, I will, I act.
By touch and kiss and six times three
I was, and am, and will not be.

So swift this sky of rain and stars!
So slow this earth of dust and scars!
When I am dead how shall I see
Where I must go that I may be?

When six times three is rain times dust,
That where I go, may I be must?
And if I dance and sing and play,
Must I go where, be that I may?
And if I sing so sharp, so flat,
Where I must go, may I be that? –
And dance and sing so low, so high,
Go where that may, must I be I?

SECOND HONEYMOON
Joanna Trollope

CHAPTER ONE

Edie put her hand out, took a breath and slowly, slowly pushed open his bedroom door. The room inside looked as if he had never left it. The bed was unmade, the curtains half-drawn, the carpet almost invisible under trails of clothing. There were single trainers on shelves, mugs and cereal bowls on the floor, scatterings of papers and books everywhere. On the walls the same posters hung haphazardly from nuggets of blue gum; a Shakespeare play from a long ago school outing, Kate Moss in a mackintosh, the Stereophonics from a concert at Earls Court. It looked, at first glance, as it had looked for a large part of his twenty-two years. It looked as if he was coming back, any minute.

Edie stepped through the chaos on the floor – ah, that's where her only bone china mug had got to – and pulled the curtains fully apart. One side, obviously accustomed to doing this, rushed headlong to the left and slid triumphantly off the pole to the floor. Edie looked up. The finial that stopped the end was missing. It had probably been missing for months, years, and Ben's solution had been simply, pragmatically really, not to touch the curtain. In fact, on reflection, he would have had to thread the curtain back on to the pole just once, when the finial first fell off, and this small sign of enterprise and efficiency on his part made Edie think that she might cry. She picked up the fallen curtain and held it hard against her, swallowing against the crying.

'He hasn't gone to Mongolia,' Russell had almost shouted at her that morning, 'He hasn't *died*. He's gone to Walthamstow.'

Edie had said nothing. She had gone on jabbing at a hermetically sealed packet of coffee with the wrong kind of knife and said nothing.

'End of a Tube line,' Russell said unnecessarily, 'That's all. Walthamstow.'

Edie flung the coffee and the knife into the sink. She would not look at Russell, she would not speak. She hated him when he was like this, when he knew perfectly well what was the matter and refused to admit it. She didn't hate his attitude, she told herself: she hated *him*.

'Sorry,' Russell said.

Edie pulled the curtain up now and covered her face with it. It smelled of dust, years and years of grimy London dust, silting in through the window frames like the fine tilth from a tea bag. She hadn't acknowledged Russell's 'sorry'. She hadn't looked at him. She had remained silent, distanced by emotion, until she heard him go out of the room and down the hallway – fumble, fumble by the coat rack – and out through the front door, letting it crash behind him the way they all had, two parents, three children, for close on twenty years. Twenty years. Almost all Ben's lifetime, almost a third of hers. You come to a house, Edie thought, pressing the dusty curtain against her eye sockets, carrying almost more life, more people than you can manage. And then, over time, almost everything you have carried in begins to leak out again, inexorably, and you are left clutching fallen curtains at ten o'clock on a Saturday morning instead of applying yourself, with all your new reserves of no longer required maternal energy, to quality leisure time.

She dropped the curtain back on to the floor. If she turned, slowly, and half closed her eyes, she could persuade herself that Ben had left his room in a mess as a signal to her that he hadn't really left it. That this notion of his to put all the essentials of his life into a duffel bag and carry it off to live with Naomi, in a spare room in her mother's flat in Walthamstow, was in truth no more than a notion. That he would begin to miss things, his childhood home, the cat, his pillow, his mother, and would see that life was not to be lived so satisfactorily anywhere else. But if she made herself open her eyes wide, really wide, and looked at the calibre of things he had left, the outgrown garments, the broken shoes, the discarded or irrelevant books and CDs and papers, she could see that what Ben had left behind was what he didn't want any more. He had taken what represented the present and the future, and he had left the past, leaving it in such a way as to emphasise its irrelevance to him. Edie bent down and began, without method or enthusiasm, to pick up the cereal bowls.

It wasn't as if Ben had ever, really, been away from home. His school days had melted comfortably into his college days and then into irregular, haphazard days of assistant to a self-employed photographer who specialised in portraits. All through these years Ben had come home, more nights than not, to sleep in the bedroom across the landing from his parents' bedroom, which had been allotted him when he was two. His bedroom had been by turns pale yellow, purple, papered with aeroplanes, and almost black. The detritus of his life, from Thomas the Tank Engine to trailing computer cables, had spilled out of his room and across the landing, symbols of his changing taste, his changing world. The thought of the order – no, not order, the absence of chaos – that might follow his departure for Walthamstow brought Edie close to panic. It was like – like having an artery shut off, a light extinguished. It was far, far worse than when Matt had gone. Or Rosa. It was far, far worse than she expected.

She began to pile mugs and bowls without method on Ben's table. He had done homework at that table, made models, hacked with blades at the edges. She sat down by it, on the chair with the broken cane seat, filled in by a gaudy Indian cushion embroidered with mirrors. She looked at the mess on the table. Ben was her youngest, her last. When the others went, she had felt a pang, but there had always been Ben, there had always been the untidy, demanding, gratifying living proof that she was doing what she was meant to do, that she was doing something no one else could do. And, if Ben wasn't there to confirm her proper perception of herself in that way, what was she going to do about the future? What was she going to do about herself?

'It's awful,' her sister Vivien had said on the telephone. 'It's just awful. You spend all these years and years developing this great supporting muscle for your children and then they just whip round, don't they, and hack it through.' She'd paused, and then she'd said, in a cooler tone, 'Actually, it's not so bad for you because you've always got the theatre.'

'I haven't,' Edie said, 'I – '

'Well, I know you aren't working at this precise moment. But you always *could* be, couldn't you? You're always going for auditions and things.'

'That,' Edie said, her voice rising, 'has nothing to do with Ben going, nothing to do with *motherhood*.'

There was another pause and then Vivien said, in the slightly victim voice Edie had known since their child-hoods, 'Eliot's gone too, Edie. And he's my only child. He's all I've got.'

Eliot had gone to Australia. He had found a job on a local radio station in Cairns, and within six months had a flat and a girlfriend there. Ben had gone five stops up the Victoria line to Walthamstow.

'OK,' Edie said to Vivien, conceding.

'I do know – '

'Yes.'

'Lovely,' Vivien said, 'for Russell.'

'Mm.'

'Having you back – '

Edie felt a flash of temper. Eliot's father, Max, had drift-ed in and out of his wife and son's life in a way that made sure that the only thing about him that was predictable was his unreliability. Vivien might be able to trump her over the pain caused by distances, but she wasn't going to trump her too over the pain caused by husbands.

'Enough,' Edie said.

'Enough,' she said to herself now, her elbows on Ben's table. She twisted round. Against the wall, Ben's bed stood exactly as he had left it, the duvet slewed towards the floor, the pillow dented, a magazine here, a pair of underpants there. It was tempting, she thought, holding hard to the chairback as an anchor, to spring up and fling herself down on Ben's bed and push her face into his pillow and breathe and breathe. It was very tempting.

Downstairs the front door crashed again. She heard Russell's feet on the tiles of the hall, heard him say something companionable to the cat.

'Edie?'

She went on staring at Ben's pillows.

'I've got the newspapers,' Russell called. 'An orgy of them — '

Edie looked up at Ben's bookshelves, at the space at the end where his teddy bear always sat, wearing Russell's old school tie from over forty years ago. The bear had gone. She stood up, holding an awkward stack of crockery.

'Coming,' she said.

The garden was one of the reasons they had bought the house twenty years ago. It was only the width of the house, but it was seventy-five feet long, long enough for Matt, then eight, to kick a ball in. It also had a shed. Russell had loved the idea of a shed, the idea of paraffin heaters and fingerless gloves and listening to the football results on an old battery operated radio. He saw seclusion in that shed, somewhere set apart from his family life and his working life because both were, by their very nature, all talk. He had a vision of being in the shed on winter weekend afternoons, probably wrapped in a sleeping bag, and looking back down the garden to the house, a dark shape with lit windows, and knowing that all that life and clamour was there for him to step back into, when he chose. It was a very luxurious vision, in that it encompassed both privacy and participation, and he clung to it during the years while the shed filled up with bikes and paint tins and broken garden chairs, leaving no space for him. It was even called "Dad's shed".

This Saturday afternoon, he told Edie, he was going to clear it out.

'Why?'

'Because it's full of useless junk.'

She was chopping things, making one of her highly coloured rough-hewn salads.

'And then?'

'Then what?'

'When you have cleared out the shed, what will you do with it?'

'Use it.'

Edie threw a handful of tomato pieces into the salad bowl.

'What for?'

Russell considered saying for reading pornography in, and decided against it. He said, 'The purpose will become plain as I clear it.'

Edie picked up a yellow pepper. She had gathered her hair on top of her head and secured it with a purple plastic comb. She looked, in some ways, about thirty. She also looked small and defiant.

'You were clearing Ben's room this morning,' Russell said gently.

'No,' Edie said.

He went over to the fridge and took out a bottle of Belgian beer. The boys would drink it straight out of the bottle. Russell went across the kitchen, behind Edie, to the cupboard where the glasses were kept.

He said, his back to her, 'What were you doing then?'

'Nothing,' Edie said. 'Thinking.'

Russell took a glass out of the cupboard. He said, his back still turned, holding the glass and the bottle, 'They just do grow up. It's what happens.'

'Yes,' Edie said.

'It's what's *meant* to happen.'

'Yes.'

Russell turned. He put down the glass and the bottle and came to stand behind her.

'He's doing what he wants to do.'

Edie sliced through the pepper.

'I know.'

'You can't – '

'I know!' Edie shouted. She flung the knife across the table. Russell moved to retrieve it. He held it out to her.

'Stop chucking things. It's so childish.'

Edie took the knife and laid it down on the chopping board with elaborate care. Then she leaned on her hands and looked down into her salad.

'I love Ben as much as you do,' Russell said, 'But he's twenty-two. He's a man. When I – '

'Please don't,' Edie said.

'I met you when I was twenty-two.'

'Twenty-three.'

'All right, then. Twenty-three. And you were twenty-one.'

'Just,' Edie said.

'I seem to remember us thinking we were quite old enough to get married.'

Edie straightened up and folded her arms.

'We'd left home. We wanted to leave home. I left home at seventeen.'

'Ben didn't.'

'He liked it here, he loved it – '

'And now he loves Naomi.'

Edie gave a little snort. Russell went back to his beer. He said, pouring it, 'This happens to everyone. Everyone with children. It started with Matt, remember. Matt left at twenty-two.'

Edie moved away from the table and leaned instead against the sink, staring out into the garden.

'You just don't think,' she said, 'that it's going to end.'

'God!' Russell said. He tried a little yelp of laughter. 'End! Does parenthood ever, *ever* end?'

Edie turned round and looked at the table.

'If you want any lunch,' she said, 'you finish that.'

'OK.'

'I'm going out.'

'Are you? Where are you going?'

'A film maybe. Sit in a café. Buy a forty-watt light bulb.'

'Edie – '

She began to walk towards the door to the hall.

'Better practise, hadn't I? For the next chapter?'

Outside the shed, Russell made a pile of things to keep, a pile of things to throw away, and a pile to ask Edie about. He had made a cheese and pickle sandwich from the last of the white sliced loaf – there would presumably be no more of those, without Ben around to indulge with them – and had eaten it sitting in a mouldy Lloyd Loom chair that had belonged to his mother, in the pale April sunshine. He would also have added a newspaper or two if the sunshine hadn't been qualified by a sharp breeze blowing intermittently through the gap between the semi-detached houses that backed on to his own. They were much grander houses than his – broad steps to the front doors, generous windows to the floor, gravelled car-parking spaces – in a much grander road, but they faced east, rather than west, so they got the wind before he did, and only early sun.

Edie wasn't back. She had returned briefly to the kitchen, wearing a cast-off denim jacket of Rosa's, and kissed his cheek. He had wanted to say something, to hold her for a moment, but had decided against it. Instead, he let her bump her face against his, fleetingly, and watched her go. The cat watched her too, from a place on the crowded dresser where he was not supposed to sit, next to the fruit bowl. When the front door slammed, the cat gave Russell a quick glance and then went back to washing. He waited half an hour after Russell went out to the garden and then he came out to see what was happening, stepping fastidiously over the damp grass. As soon as Russell left the Lloyd Loom chair, he leaped into it and sat there, watching, his tail curled trimly round his paws and his expression inscrutable.

He was really Ben's cat. Ben had been the only one of their children who had longed for an animal, who had badgered on about everything from a hippo to a hamster until, on his tenth birthday, Russell had gone to a dingy pet shop somewhere in Finsbury Park, and come home with a tabby kitten in a wire basket. Ben called the kitten Arsenal, after his chosen football club, and remained indifferent to the implications of this being inevitably shortened to Arsie. Arsie was now twelve and cool as a tulip.

'Look,' Russell said to Arsie, 'Rosa's tricycle. She loved that.'

Arsie looked unmoved. Rosa's tricycle, once metallic lilac with a white plastic basket on the front, was now mostly rust.

'Keep or chuck?' Russell said.

Arsie yawned.

'Chuck,' Russell said. 'Chuck, but inform Rosa.'

He crouched and inspected the tricycle. Rosa had stuck stickers everywhere, glitter stickers of cartoon animals and fairies. She had looked sweet on that tricycle, pedalling furiously, straight red hair flapping, the white plastic basket crammed with all the stuffed animals she carried everywhere, lining them up at meals round her place, putting them in a circle round her pillow. Sometimes when he looked at her now, twenty-six years old and working for a PR company, he caught a glimpse of the child on the tricycle, like a ghost in a mirror. She had been a turbulent little girl full of noise and purpose. Some of the noise and purpose were still there, but the turbulence had translated itself into something closer to emotional volatility, a propensity to swerve crazily in and out of relationships. At least one had to be thankful that she did swerve out again, particularly in the case of the appalling Josh.

Russell straightened up and looked at the house. Rosa's window was on the top floor, on the left. Since Rosa had left home, they'd had the odd lodger in that room, and in Matt's, next to it; drama students Edie was teaching or impoverished actors she'd once been in repertory with who had small parts in plays in little North London theatres. They were good lodgers on the whole, never awake too early, never short of something to say, and they provided, unconsciously, the perfect excuse to postpone any decision about moving to something smaller. The house might be shabby, in places very shabby, but it was not something Russell could imagine being without. It was, quite simply, a given in his life, in their lives, the result of being left a miraculous small legacy in his twenties, when he and Edie were living in a dank flat, with two children and a baby, above an ironmongers off the Balls Pond Road.

'Four bedrooms,' Edie had said, whispering as if the house could hear her. 'What'll we ever do with four bedrooms?'

It had been in a terrible state, of course, damp and neglected, with mushrooms up the stairwell and a hole in the roof you could see the stars through. But somehow, then, with Edie enjoying a steady spell of television work, and the agency getting going, the house had seemed to them needy rather than daunting, more theirs, somehow, because it was crying out for rescue. They had no kitchen for a year, no finished bathroom for two, no carpets for five. Matt wore gumboots all his childhood, from the moment he got out of bed. It was perhaps no surprise that Matt should turn out to be the most orthodox of their children, the one with an electronic diary and polished shoes. When he came home, he was inclined to point out that the crack in the sitting-room ceiling was lengthening, that the smell of damp in the downstairs lavatory was not just a smell, that regular outside painting was a sound investment.

'It's hard,' Russell said, 'for us old bohemians to get worked up about such things.'

'Then listen to me,' Matt said.

He said that often, now. He had started saying it after he left home, and returned, just for occasional meals, with a newly critical eye. 'Listen to me,' he'd say to Edie about a part she was reading for, to Russell about some new direction the agency might take, to Ben about his 'A' level choices.

'You're so adult,' Edie would say, looking at him fondly. 'I love it.'

She loved it, of course, because she didn't listen to him. She loved it the way she loved his regular haircuts and well-mannered clothes and competence with technology. It was amusing to her, and endearing, to see this well put together grown man in her kitchen, explaining to her how to send text messages on her mobile phone, and visualise him, simultaneously, once asleep in his cot or sitting, reading earnestly on his potty. She could play games like that, Russell thought, because she still had Ben; the security of Ben gave her the licence not to take Matt seriously, not to see his maturity as anything other than sweet play-acting.

If Matt was irritated by her attitude, he gave no sign. He treated her as he had always treated both his parents, as very well-meaning people of whom he was fond and who he needed to take practical care of because they seemed to decline to do it for themselves. It was plain he thought Edie indulged Ben, just as it was plain he thought Rose indulged herself, but he kept these opinions to their proper place, on the edges of his own rightly preoccupying life. He worked for a mobile telephone company, had a girlfriend with a job in the City, and with whom he shared a flat. He was entitled, Russell thought, inspecting a neat stack of broken lampshades and wondering why they had ever been considered worthy of salvage, to say, every so often, and to a family who lived so much more carelessly than he did, 'Listen to me.'

Russell did listen. He might not often take advice, but he listened. He had listened while Matt had explained, at tremendous length one evening in a cramped bar in Covent Garden, that Russell should specialise. Matt described his father's agency, which represented actors who were particularly interested in film and television work, as 'limping along'. Russell, nursing a glass of red wine, had been mildly affronted. After the next glass, he had felt less affronted. After the third glass, Matt's proposal that Russell should specialise in providing actors for advertising voice-over work seemed less alien, less unattractively practical than it had an hour before.

'I know it's not theatre,' Matt had said. 'But it's money.'

'It's *all* about money!' Edie had cried, two hours later, brushing her teeth, 'Isn't it? That's all it's about!'

'Possibly,' Russell said carefully, 'it has to be.'

'It's sordid. It's squalid. Where's the acting in bouncing on sofas?'

'Not bouncing on them. Talking about them.'

Edie spat into the basin.

'Well, if you can *bring* yourself – '

'I rather think I can.'

'Well, just don't ask *me*.'

Russell let a pause fall. He climbed into bed and picked up his book, a biography of Alexander the Great. He put his glasses on.

'No,' he said, 'no. I rather think I shan't.'

Since 1975, Russell Boyd Associates (there were none) had occupied three attic rooms behind Shaftesbury Avenue. For almost thirty years, Russell had worked in a room which had undoubtedly been a maid's bedroom long ago. It had a dormer window and sloping ceilings and was carpeted with the Turkey carpet that had once been in Russell's grandparents dining room in Hull, now worn to a grey blur of weft cotton threads, garnished here and there with a few brave remaining tufts of red and blue and green. Matt, encouraged by Russell's acceptance of his advice about the agency, then tried to persuade him to modernise the office, to put down a wooden floor and install halogen lights on gleaming metal tracks.

'No,' Russell said.

'But Dad – '

'I like it. I like it just as it is. So do my clients.'

Matt had kicked at piles of straining cardboard folders piled like old bolsters against the bookshelves.

'It's awful. It's like your old shed.'

Russell looked now, at his shed. It was half-empty, but what remained looked intractable, as if prepared to resist movement. Arsie had left the chair and returned to the house and the sun had sunk behind the houses leaving a raw dankness instead. He glanced down at Rosa's tricycle, on its side in the stack to be discarded.

'Rosa's bike,' she had always called it. Not 'mine' but 'Rosa's'.

'Russell!' Edie called.

He raised his head. She was standing at the corner of the house, where the side door to the kitchen was. She had Arsie in her arms.

'Tea!' Edie shouted.

'Look,' Edie said, 'I'm sorry.'

She had made tea in the big pot with cabbage roses on it. It was extremely vulgar but it had intense associations for Edie, as everything in her life did, everything that reminded her of a place, a person, a happening. She said,

'I was fed up with you because you wouldn't understand.'

'I do understand,' Russell said.

'Do you?'

He nodded, tensing slightly.

'Then tell me,' Edie demanded. 'Explain what is the matter.'

Russell paused. Then he said, 'It's the end of a particularly compelling – and urgent – phase of motherhood. And it's very hard to adjust to.'

'I don't want to adjust,' Edie said. She poured tea into the huge cracked blue cups she had found in a junk shop in Scarborough, touring with – what was it? A Priestley play perhaps.

'I want Ben back,' Edie said.

Russell poured milk into his tea.

'I want him back,' Edie said fiercely, 'I want him back to make me laugh and infuriate me and exploit me and make me feel *necessary*.'

Russell picked up his teacup and held it, cradling it in his palms. The aroma of the tea rose up to him, making him think of his grandmother. She had saved Darjeeling tea for Sundays. 'The champagne of teas,' she said, every time she drank it.

'Are you listening?' Edie said.

'Yes,' he said, 'But you forget I know.'

She leaned forward.

'How do I make you *mind*?'

'Good question.'

'What?'

He put his cup down. He said, seriously, not looking at her, 'How do I make *you* mind?'

She stared.

'What?' she said again.

'I've been out there,' Russell said, 'for about three hours, I've been sifting through all sorts of rubbish, things that mattered once and don't any more. And that's quite painful, knowing things won't come again, knowing things are over for ever.'

'But – '

'Wait,' Russell said, 'Just *wait*. Rosa's not going to ride that trike again, Matt's not going to hit with that bat, you're not going to read under that lampshade. That's not comfortable, that's not easy to know, to have to accept. But we have to, because we have no choice. And we also have something left.'

Edie took a long swallow of tea and looked at him over the rim of her cup.

'Yes?'

'You talk about wanting Ben back. You talk about his energy and neediness and the way that makes you feel. Well, just think for a moment about how *I* feel. I didn't marry you in order to have Matt and Rosa and Ben, though I'm thankful we did. I married you because I wanted to be with you, because you somehow make things shine for me, even when you're horrible. You want Ben back. Well, you'll have to deal with that as best you can. And while you're dealing with it, I'll give you something else to think about, something that isn't going to go away. Edie – I want you back. I was here before the children and I'm here now.' He put his cup down with finality. 'And I'm not going away.'

UNTITLED NOVEL
Scott Turow

ALL PARENTS KEEP SECRETS

All parents keep secrets from their children. My father kept more than most.

Dad passed away in 2001 at the age of eighty-six, the result of what the doctor called multi-system failure – heart disease, lung cancer and emphysema – which could have been short-handed as sixty years of cigarettes. In a characteristic demonstration of resolve, my mother refused to leave the burial details to my sister and me, and insisted on meeting the funeral director with us. She chose a casket big enough to require a hood ornament, then pondered each word as the mortician read out the proposed death announcement.

'Was David a veteran?' he asked. The undertaker was the cleanest-looking man I'd ever seen, with lacquered nails, shaped eyebrows and a face so smooth I suspected electrolysis.

'World War II,' barked my sister. Sarah always seems to hear the ticking of the hours she's not billing at her accounting firm in Oakland.

The funeral director showed us the black icon of a waving stars and stripes that would appear in the paper beside Dad's name, but my mother was already fiercely shaking her thinning grey curls.

'No,' she said. 'No war. No flag. War he never liked.' When she was upset, Mom's English tended to fail her. And my sister and I both knew enough not to temporise when she was in such moods. The war, except for the bare details of how my father, an American officer, and my mother, an inmate in a German concentration camp, had fallen in love in moments, had been throughout our lives an unpleasantness too great for discussion. But I had always assumed the silence was for her sake, not his.

My mother is not the kind to put things off, and by the last day of the mourning visitation, she made it clear that she was ready to start sorting through Dad's belongings. Sarah announced she was too pressed to participate and headed back to Oakland, no doubt feeling that she'd scored once more in her endless competition with me, by underscoring the poignant contrast to her big brother, an unemployed schlep.

Sadly available, I was put to work in my father's closet on Monday morning. Although my mother insisted that I consider taking much of his clothing, it was a laughable illusion to think any of it could fit my swollen form. I selected a few ties to make her happy and began boxing the rest of his old shirts and suits, most disastrously out of fashion, for donation to the Haven, the Jewish relief agency where my mother had worked as the volunteer director for nearly twenty years.

But I was unprepared for the emotion that swept over me as I worked. I knew my father as a remote, circumspect man, very orderly in almost everything, good with his hands, studious, kind. He preferred work to social engagements. In any crowd, he was the sort who stood around with his fists jammed in his pockets without much to say. In most things, he accepted my mother's direction, only very rarely allowing himself an open sigh as a form of protest.

The Talmud says that a father should draw a son close with one hand and push him away with the other. Dad basically failed on both accounts. I felt a steadiness in his affection, but found him elusive at the core. As a kid, my father's reserve, dignified though it often was, tended to infuriate me. My mother hovered, overwhelmed even. He never really would have stood a chance against her – no one ever has – but he seemed to have checked out entirely. I have an omnipresent memory of the times I was alone with him in the house and being maddened by the total silence. Did he even know I was there?

Now that he was gone, I was intensely aware of everything I'd never settled with him – in fact, in many cases, never even started on. Was he sorry I was not a lawyer like him? What did he make of my daughters? Did he think the world was a good place or bad, and how could he explain the fact that the Trappers, for whom he maintained a resilient passion, had never won the World Series in his lifetime? Children and parents never get it all sorted out. Some questions I would have to answer on my own. But it was painful to find that even in death he remained so enigmatic.

And so this business of touching the things my father touched, of smelling his scents of Mennan talcum powder and Canoe aftershave, left me periodically swamped by feelings of longing and absence. Handling his personal effects was an intimacy I would never have been permitted were he alive. I was in pain but deeply moved and wept

SCOTT TUROW

freely. My mother, being herself, feigned not to notice. At one point she took a few steps into the room, only to find me dragging the back of my hand across my nose, like a six year old.

'Oh,' she said, as she stared at me, her very round peg of a boy who had never quite found a space in the world to fit him. She herself was yet to shed a tear and undoubtedly thought that kind of fierce stoicism was more appropriate to a man of fifty-three. Then again, it had long been silently acknowledged that my life was disappointment to both of us. 'I thought it was a cat,' she said and quickly departed.

With the clothing packed, I began looking through the pillar of cardboard boxes in the dim far corner of the closet. It was a remarkable collection of things I ultimately found within them, marked by a sentimentality I always thought Dad lacked. He had kept the schmaltzy valentines Sarah and I had made for him as grade school art projects and the medal he'd won in high school as the tri-counties best back-stroker. There were dozens of packets of darkening Kodachromes reflecting the life of his young family, and several private files from his years in the general counsel's office at Moreland Insurance. In the bottom box, I found memorabilia of the War, lots of papers, several Nazi insignia taken, I imagined, as war trophies, and dozens of two by two black-and-white snaps that revealed an outstanding photographic eye, albeit someone else's since my father was often in the picture looking thin and stoical. Finally, there was a bundle of letters packed in an old candy tin to which a note was tied with a piece of green yarn dulled by time. It was dated in July, 1945.

Dear David,
I am returning to your family the letters you have written

224

to me while you have been overseas. I suppose they may mean something to you in the future. As you are determined no longer to be a part of my life, I have to accept that as time goes on, and my hurt diminishes, they will no longer mean anything to me. I'm sure your father has told you that I brought your ring back to him last month. I will avoid repeating the spiteful advice my parents and sisters have provided me. For all of this, David, I can't make myself be angry at you for ending our engagement. When I saw your father, he said that you were now being court-martialed and face prison! I can hardly believe that about someone like you, but I would never have believed that you would desert me like this either. My father says men are known to go crazy during wartime. But I can't wait for you to come back to your senses.

When I cry at night, David, and I won't pretend for your sake that I don't, one thing bothers me more than anything else. I spent so many hours praying to God for him to deliver you safely; I begged him to allow you to live, and if he was especially kind, to let you to come back whole, although that was never a requirement on my part. Now that the fighting is over, I cannot believe that my prayers were answered and that I was fool enough to never ask that when you came home, you would be coming home to me.

I wish you the best of luck in your present troubles.

Grace

This letter knocked me flat. Court-martialed! Engaged! I had never heard a word of any of that. But even more than my surprise, across the arc of time, like light emitted by distant stars decades before, I was lacerated by this woman's pain. I shared so much of her confusion, her disappointment and misplaced love. For her sake, as much as my own, I felt an instant and ferocious curiosity to find out what had occurred.

My Dad's death had come at what was already a very hard time for me. I had been separated for eighteen months from Nona, my high school sweetheart and wife of three decades, and then only nine weeks before I had been sacked by the Kindle County *Tribune,* where I had worked as a reporter since the day I graduated from the U., thirty-five years ago. I wish my so-called 'early retirement' from the *Trib* had been a shock, but the handwriting had been on the wall so long that I had begun to regard it as part of the decorating, and I had already begun giving given some thought to what I would do when the hammer fell. Like most out of work journalists, I said I was going to write a book, and had played around with several ideas, including a history of the Kindle River, and a reinvestigation of a murder case, now nearly two decades old, where the Chief Deputy Prosecutor had been acquitted of the murder of a colleague. Yet after a couple of months of unemployment, I could not claim to be doing much but farting around.

But with the discovery of my father's unknown past, especially the fact that he had endured a general court martial, I finally had a subject. His secret offered not only intrigue, but the chance to solve a persistent riddle, for the truth was that from the time I was a kid I sensed that something had *happened* to my father. Although it was my mother who is referred to in contemporary parlance as 'a survivor', it was he who much more clearly reflected a traumatic past. There was a bewildered air that overcame him from time to time, an unnerved stillness in his eyes, while a finger or his foot tapped restively and his posture became drawn, wilted by the power of some recollection that had fully removed him from the present. And there was something foreign in his restraint, as if God or someone else always had a hand upon his shoulder. Family members sometimes commented that as a younger man he had been more outspoken. My grandmother's theory, which she rarely kept to herself, was that Gilda, my mother, had largely taken David's tongue by always speaking first and with such authority.

Simply put, he was not a person at ease with himself. He used alcohol as a sedative. In the common sense of the term, he was not a drunk, but he had three scotches every night, one an hour from eight p.m. to ten p.m., because he said it was the only way he could get some sleep. There was often another drink when he woke, as he inevitably did, in the middle of the night, seized from sleep by turbulent dreams. Although he rarely lost his temper with either my sister or me, when he did, he was moved to a sputtering fury. Once he saw me larking on my bike with friends and, as a result, nearly get run over when a car screamed around the corner. He snatched me up by one arm from the pavement where I lay and carried me that way until he could throw me down on the parkway. Even so young, I understood he was somehow angrier about the panic I'd caused him than the danger I'd posed to myself. Despite my grief at his passing, I sensed that for him a long struggle was finally over.

Now the chance perhaps to find out what had so troubled him inspired me. I filled out innumerable government forms and crossed the continent several times, to visit the Army War College in Pennsylvania, the JAG School Library in Charlottesville, the Pentagon Library, Fort McNair which houses the Army's Center on Military History and several sites of the National Records Center. I also found myself at a number of spots in Connecticut in my efforts to reassemble the records of Barrington Leach, the JAG Lt Colonel who defended my father – unsuccessfully, it turned out – at his trial. I hectored relatives for recollections and managed to get several to plumb their basements and attics for photographs and letters and other papers. In time I learned that my father's general court-martial was the only one brought in World War II against someone who was himself a Judge Advocate, perhaps explaining the harshness of the sentence he initially received – five years at hard labor.

And so learning my father's story and telling it gripped me in the way no journalistic enterprise ever had. Always battling a tendency to sloth, I worked happily sixteen or eighteen hours a day. I regarded the dark corridors of libraries and archives as my happy hunting ground. This was going to make not only a book, but *my* book, and a great book, a book which, like the corniest *deus ex machina* would rescue my life from the shadows that had long fallen over it. And then, like the cross-examiners in the criminal courtrooms I covered for so many years, I made the cardinal mistake, asked one question too many and discovered the single fact, the only conceivable detail that could scoop me of my father's story.

He had written it himself.

ABOUT THE AUTHORS

MARGARET ATWOOD's books have been published in over thirty-five countries. She is the author of more than thirty works, which include fiction, poetry and critical essays. Of her novels, *The Handmaid's Tale*, *Cat's Eye*, *Alias Grace* and her most recent novel *Oryx and Crake* were shortlisted for the Booker Prize, and *Alias Grace* also won the Giller Prize in Canada and the Premio Mondello in Italy. *The Blind Assassin* won the 2000 Booker Prize. She lives in Toronto with writer Graeme Gibson.

MAEVE BINCHY was born in Co. Dublin and studied history at UCD. In 1969 she joined the *Irish Times*. For some ten years she was based in London writing humorous columns from all over the world, before returning to Ireland where she now lives with her husband, writer Gordon Snell. She is the author of several volumes of short stories, among them *London Transports*, *Dublin 4*, *The Lilac Bus* (which has been filmed for television) and *Silver Wedding*. Her novels include *Light a Penny Candle*, *Echoes* (the TV adaptation of which has been shown throughout the world), *Firefly Summer*, *Circle of Friends*, (which became a motion picture starring Chris O'Donnell and Minnie Driver), *The Copper Beech*, *The Glass Lake*,

Evening Class, Tara Road (currently being filmed in Ireland and South Africa), *Aches and Pains* (illustrated by Wendy Shea), and *Scarlet Feather* and *Quentins*, both of which spent many weeks on the bestseller lists on both sides of the Atlantic. Her latest bestseller is *Nights of Rain and Stars*. She was awarded the Lifetime Achievement award at the British Book Awards in 1999. For more information see www.maevebinchy.com.

TRACY CHEVALIER was born and grew up in Washington, DC. She moved to England in 1984 and worked as a reference-book editor. In 1993 she took an MA in Creative Writing at the University of East Anglia and her first novel, *The Virgin Blue*, was published in 1997. She is the author of three further novels: *Girl with a Pearl Earring*, *Falling Angels* and *The Lady and the Unicorn*. She is currently researching and writing her fifth novel, which will be about the painter and poet William Blake. Tracy Chevalier lives in London with her husband and their son.

HARLAN COBEN has won the Edgar Award, Shamus Award and Anthony Award – the first author to win all three. His most recent novels, *Just One Look*, *No Second Chance*, *Tell No One* and *Gone For Good* are international bestsellers. His books are published in more than twenty-eight languages in over thirty countries. His latest thriller, *No Second Chance*, is the first International Book of the Month Club pick – the main selection for book clubs in fifteen countries. Since his critically-acclaimed Myron Bolitar series debuted in 1995, Harlan Coben has won the Mystery Writers of America's Edgar Allan Poe Award and was nominated for the Edgar two other times. He also won the Anthony Award at the World Mystery

Conference and the Shamus Award by the Private Eye Writers of America. His novel *One False Move* earned him the WH Smith Fresh Talent Award. The novel *Tell No One* was short-listed for an Edgar, a Macavity, an Anthony and a Barry Award and won Le Grand Prix des Lectrics de Elle. *Gone for Good* won the WH Smith Thumping Good Read Award. Coben was the first writer in more than a decade to be invited to write fiction for the *New York Times* op-ed page. Seven novels in the Myron Bolitar series are now in print. Harlan was born in Newark, New Jersey and lives in New Jersey with his wife, Anne Armstrong-Coben MD, medical director of Covenant House in Newark, and their four children.

Born in Brazil, PAULO COELHO is one of the most beloved storytellers of our time, renowned for his international bestsellers *The Alchemist* and *Eleven Minutes*. His books have been translated into fifty-nine languages and published in 150 countries. He is also the recipient of numerous prestigious international awards, among them the Crystal Award by the World Economic Forum, France's Chevalier de l'Ordre National de la Légion d'Honneur, and Germany's Bambi 2001 Award. He was inducted at the Brazilian Academy of Letters in 2002. Paulo Coelho writes a weekly column syndicated throughout the world. For further information, please see www.paulocoelho.com and www.santjordi-asociados.com.

J. M. COETZEE was born in South Africa in 1940 and educated in South Africa and the United States. He is the author of eight works of fiction, four collections of essays, and several works of indeterminate genre, as well as of translations from the Dutch and Afrikaans. Among the literary prizes he has won are the Booker Prize (twice), the Commonwealth Prize, and the Jerusalem Prize. He won the Nobel Prize for Literature in 2003. He lives in Australia.

NICHOLAS EVANS was born in 1950 in Worcestershire and read Law at Oxford. During the 1970s he trained as a journalist and then a TV reporter, specialising in US politics and foreign affairs, most notably covering the war in Beirut. By the 1980s he was at London Weekend Television, producing award-winning films on Laurence Olivier, Francis Bacon and David Hockney for the *South Bank Show*. His film on director David Lean proved a turning point. Lean became a friend and mentor, encouraging him to start writing and producing independently of LWT. His credits as a screenwriter and film producer include *Murder by the Book*, *Act of Betrayal*, *Secret Weapon* and *Just Like A Woman*. Nicholas Evans' first novel, *The Horse Whisperer*, has sold more than ten million copies worldwide since its publication in 1995 and has been translated into a total of thirty-six languages. It was made into the biggest Hollywood film of 1998, produced, directed by and starring Robert Redford. His following novels, *The Loop* and *The Smoke Jumper*, were also international bestsellers.

MARK HADDON is a writer for television and radio as well as a bestselling novelist. His television credits include *The Wild House*, *Microsoap*, *Starstreet* and *Fungus the Bogeyman*. His radio plays include *1,000 Ships* and *Coming Down the Mountain* for the Radio 4 Afternoon Play. His broadcasting awards include, among others, a Royal Television Society award, a New York TV Festival Gold Award and two BAFTAs. He has written many books for children including *Gilbert's Gobstopper*, *A Narrow Escape for Princess Sharon*, *Tony and the Tomato Soup*, *Titch Johnson – Almost World Champion* and the *Agent Z* series. His breakthrough into the adult market came with the bestselling novel *The Curious Incident of the Dog in the Night-Time* which has been translated in thirty-five languages so far, and the film rights have been sold. Awards for the novel include the Whitbread Book of the Year Award, the *Guardian* Children's Fiction Prize, the Commonwealth Writers Prize, WH Smith Children's Book of the Year, Waterstone's Literary Fiction Award, and many others. He has also published poetry and has worked as a cartoonist for, among others, the *New Statesman*, the *Spectator*, *Private Eye*, the *Sunday Telegraph* and the *Guardian* for whom he co-wrote a cartoon-strip, *Men – A User's Guide*.

NICK HORNBY was born in Redhill, Surrey, in 1957 and is a graduate of Cambridge University where he read English. He has regularly contributed to *Esquire*, the *Sunday Times*, *Time Out*, the *Literary Review*, the *New Yorker* and the *Independent* writing chiefly on books, sports and pop culture, and has written features for *GQ*, *Elle*, *Time*, *Vogue* and McSweeney's monthly magazine *The Believer* where he has a monthly column, 'Stuff I've Been Reading'. His first book, *Contemporary American Fiction*, was published in 1992 and his memoir, *Fever Pitch*, was released the same year which won the William Hill Sports Book of the Year Award and was adapted as both a play and a film. The international bestselling novels *High Fidelity* and *About a Boy* were successfully adapted into hit films. *How to Be Good*, his third novel, won the WH Smith Award for Fiction. He edited an anthology of stories called

Speaking with the Angel (2000), sales of which benefit TreeHouse, a national educational charity for children with autism. *31 Songs* (US title *Songbook*) was short-listed for the prestigious National Book Critics Circle Award in the USA. In 1999 he was awarded the E. M. Forster Award by the American Academy of Arts and Letters. In 2003 he won the Writers' Writer Award at the Orange Word International Writers Festival. He lives and works in Highbury, North London.

MARIAN KEYES is the internationally bestselling author of *Watermelon*, *Lucy Sullivan is Getting Married*, *Rachel's Holiday*, *Last Chance Saloon*, *Sushi for Beginners*, *Angels* and most recently *The Other Side of the Story*, a *Sunday Times* number-one bestseller. She is published in twenty-nine different languages. A collection of her journalism, called *Under the Duvet*, is also available. Marian lives in Dublin with her husband.

STEPHEN KING is the author of more than forty worldwide bestsellers, including *Misery*, *The Green Mile*, *Bag of Bones*, and *Dreamcatcher*. Most recently, he completed his *Dark Tower* series, which he began writing in 1970. King has also published numerous collections of short stories, myriad screenplays for film and television, and several books of non-fiction, including *On Writing*. He has received the Nebula, World Fantasy, Bram Stoker and O. Henry Awards. In 2003, King was given the National Book Foundation's Medal for Distinguished Contribution to American Letters.

ALEXANDER McCALL SMITH was born in Zimbabwe in 1948 and was educated there and in Scotland.

He is married with two daughters and is professor of Medical Law at the University of Edinburgh. He is also the author of over fifty books ranging from specialist titles such as *Forensic Aspects of Sleep* to *The Perfect Hamburger* (a children's novel). In 1999 *The No. 1 Ladies' Detective Agency* was published and received two Booker Judges' Special Recommendations, was voted one of the 'International Books of the Year and the Millennium' by the *Times Literary Supplement*. Sales of the series exceed three million in the US alone and translation rights have so far been sold in thirty countries. *The Sunday Philosophy Club* saw the start of a new series of novels and a BBC television adaptation is underway. The author is also writing a novel, *44 Scotland Street*, in daily serial form for the *Scotsman*. Winner of three Author of the Year awards in 2004, Professor McCall Smith has served as Vice-Chairman of the Human Genetics Commission of the United Kingdom; a member of the International Bioethics Commission of UNESCO; Chairman of the Ethics Committee of the British Medical Journal and Chairman of the Ethics Committee of the Roslin Institute.

Born in 1948, IAN MCEWAN graduated from Sussex University and went on to do an MA course in creative writing at East Anglia under the direction of Malcolm Bradbury and Angus Wilson. His first short story, 'Homemade', was accepted by the *New American Review*. In 1975 his volume of short stories *First Love, Last Rites* was published and won the Somerset Maugham Award. In 1978, his second collection of stories *In Between the Sheets* was published, as was *The Cement Garden*, his first novel, to great acclaim. In 1979, his television play *Solid Geometry* made the headlines when the BBC banned it. In

1980, the BBC production of *The Imitation Game* gained instant recognition. In 1981, his second novel *The Comfort of Strangers* was shortlisted for the Booker Prize. His other novels include *The Child in Time* which won the Whitbread Award for best novel, *The Innocent, Black Dogs, Enduring Love* which was made into a film released in 2004 and *Amsterdam* which won the Booker Prize. *Atonement* was published in 2002, was shortlisted for the Booker Prize and went on to be a huge bestseller in both hardback and paperback.

VIKRAM SETH was born in 1952. He trained as an economist and has lived for several years each in England, California, China and India. He is the author of *The Golden Gate: A Novel In Verse, From Heaven Lake: Travels Through Sinkiang And Tibet, A Suitable Boy, Arion and the Dolphin* (a libretto), and four volumes of poetry, including *Beastly Tales*.

Author of eagerly awaited and sparklingly readable novels often centred around the domestic nuances and dilemmas of life in contemporary England, JOANNA TROLLOPE is also the author of a number of historical novels and of *Britannia's Daughters*, a study of women in the British Empire. In 1988 she wrote her first contemporary novel, *The Choir*, and this was followed by *A Village Affair, A Passionate Man, The Rector's Wife, The Men and The Girls, A Spanish Lover, The Best of Friends, Next of Kin, Other People's Children, Marrying the Mistress, Girl From the South* and, most recently, *Brother and Sister*. She lives in London and Gloucestershire.

SCOTT TUROW is a writer and attorney. He is the author of six bestselling novels, including his first, *Presumed Innocent* (1987) and his most recent novel, *Reversible Errors* published in 2002. He has also written two non-fiction books: *One L* about his experience as a law student, and his newest book, *Ultimate Punishment*, a reflection on capital punishment. Turow has been a partner in the Chicago office of Sonnenschein Nath and Rosenthal, a national law firm, since 1986, concentrating on white-collar criminal defense, while also devoting a substantial part of his time to *pro bono* matters. He has served on a number of public bodies, including the Illinois Commission on Capital Punishment appointed by Governor George Ryan in 2000 to recommend reforms to Illinois's death penalty system. Scott Turow is currently the Chairman of Illinois's Executive Ethics Commission regulating executive branch employees. He is also a past president of the Authors Guild, and is currently a trustee of Amherst College.

ACKNOWLEDGEMENTS

Thanks to the following for their generous help:
The authors, and their agents and publishers
Nicola Barr
Polly Napper
DHL Express
Macmillan Distribution Ltd
Clays Ltd, St Ives plc
Quadracolor Ltd
Creations Point of Sale
Total Media
Parallel
Allen & Unwin
Berlin Verlag
And all the UK booktrade, wholesalers and supermarkets
who have supported this book.

Stories from *The Tent* by Margaret Atwood, © O. W.
Toad Ltd, 2005, by kind permission of Bloomsbury (UK),
Doubleday (US) and McClelland & Stewart (Canada).
'Georgia Hall' by Maeve Binchy, © Maeve Binchy, 2005,
by kind permission of the author.
Copyright © 2005 by Harlan Coben from *The Innocent* by
kind permission of Orion Books (UK) and Dutton (US).

Copyright © Paulo Coelho from *The Zahir* by kind permission of HarperCollins (UK, Australia, US and Canada).

Copyright © J. M. Coetzee, 2005 from *Slow Man* by kind permission of Secker & Warburg (UK and Commonwealth) and Viking (US).

From an untitled novel by Tracy Chevalier. Copyright © Tracy Chevalier, 2005. By kind permission of HarperCollins (UK) and Dutton (US).

Copyright © 2005 by Nicholas Evans from *The Divide* by kind permission of Transworld Publishers (UK), Penguin Putnam (US) and C. Bertelsmann.

From a novel in progress by Mark Haddon, copyright © Mark Haddon, 2005. By kind permission of the author.

From *A Long Way Down* by Nick Hornby, © Nick Hornby, 2005 by kind permission of Penguin Books (UK and Canada) and Riverhead Books (US).

Copyright © 2005 by Marian Keyes from *If You Were Me* by permission of Penguin Books (UK), Poolbeg Press (Ireland) and William Morrow (US).

Copyright © 2004 by Stephen King, excerpted from the opening of a novel tentatively entitled *Lisey's Story*, as yet unscheduled for publication. The excerpt first appeared in *McSweeney's Enchanted Chamber of Astonishing Stories*, edited by Michael Chabon and published by Vintage (US and Canada).

Copyright © 2005 by Alexander McCall Smith from *Friends, Lovers, Chocolate* by kind permission of Little, Brown (UK), Pantheon Books (US) and Knopf (Canada).

Quotation from 'To Robert Fergusson' by Robert Garioch reprinted by kind permission of Birlinn.

From *Saturday* by Ian McEwan, copyright © Ian McEwan, 2005, by kind permission of Jonathan Cape

ACKNOWLEDGEMENTS

(UK), Doubleday (US) and Knopf (Canada).

'Earth and Sky' by Vikram Seth © Vikram Seth, 2005, by kind permission of the author.

From *Second Honeymoon* by Joanna Trollope, copyright © Joanna Trollope, 2005. By permission of Bloomsbury (UK and US).

Copyright © 2005 by Scott Turow, from an as yet untitled novel. By kind permission of the author.

A NOTE ON THE TYPE

The text of this book is set in Monotype Sabon,
named after the type founder, Jacques Sabon. It was
designed by Jan Tschichold and jointly developed
by Linotype, Monotype, and Stempel, in response
to a need for a typeface to be available in identical
form for mechanical hot metal composition and
hand composition using foundry type. Tschichold
based his design for Sabon roman on a font
engraved by Garamond, and Sabon italic on
a font by Granjon. It was first used in 1966 and
has proved an enduring modern classic.